Creating Happiness

Start living your best life.

Al Dorais
BBA, MSc

 FriesenPress

Suite 300 - 990 Fort St
Victoria, BC, V8V 3K2
Canada

www.friesenpress.com

Copyright © 2020 by Al Dorais
First Edition — 2020

The author has tried to recreate events, locales, and conversations from memory. In order to maintain their anonymity or preserve privacy, some names or details may have been changed. No libel, defamation, or slander is intended by the author's sharing of his experiences.

All rights reserved.

No part of this publication may be reproduced in any form, or by any means, electronic or mechanical, including photocopying, recording, or any information browsing, storage, or retrieval system, without permission in writing from FriesenPress.

ISBN
978-1-9991136-1-2 (Hardcover)
978-1-9991136-0-5 (Paperback)
978-1-9991136-2-9 (eBook)

1. SELF-HELP, MOTIVATIONAL & INSPIRATIONAL

Distributed to the trade by The Ingram Book Company

Contents

How to Use This Book 1
Introduction 5
In Pursuit of Happiness 9
Life Is a Game 19
Karma 29
Seek Joy/Avoid Pain 39
Our Brains and Computers 49
The Power of Words 61
It's Magical 69
Love: The Ultimate Power 79
Objectives vs Expectations 87
Your Purpose 99
Happiness 109
Gratitude 127
Conclusion 133
Acknowledgement 137
A Brief History 139
Exhibit A – The Lesson of the Concubines 151
Exhibit B – The Seven Pots of Gold 154
Exhibit C – Speech by Michel Caron December 2010 ... 156
Exhibit D – Who is Who 166

"Give me six hours to chop down a tree and I will spend the first four sharpening the axe."

Abraham Lincoln

How to Use This Book

I HOPE THIS BOOK WILL sharpen your axe and give you some tools you will build on during your quest toward happiness.

Keeping in mind that most who will read this book work for a living or are busy at home and the amount of time that can be dedicated to reading is scarce at times, I have structured the book in a way that gives readers options to speed up the reading process.

Except for the introduction, the first chapter, and of course the conclusion, each chapter is structured independently and therefore can be read in just about any order. Hence at times, you may have a feeling of déjà vu, but this is necessary to keep the chapters independent.

At the end of each chapter I have summarized the text for those who are reading out of sequence. You may find that the most important chapters are "Life is a Game," "Objectives vs Expectations," and "Happiness."

The first page of each chapter contains a thought or quote. This is to give the reader the opportunity to reflect on the topic before diving in. Take a minute to ponder the quote, it will pay off.

In the spirit of keeping the topic in the forefront, I have kept information on my personal background at the end of the book, the reason being that I wanted to truly explore happiness more than tinting the book with my personal story. But for the readers who like to know the writer before reading their work, I suggest that you start by reading "A Brief History" (the last chapter).

I have put my heart and soul into this book in the spirit of helping at least one person in the process. It is written as if I could send it back in time to myself, as a guideline on how to go through life being happy...most of the time.

No matter how you decide to go about reading the book, I assure you that it will be worth your time and effort.

Creating Happiness is the basis for the company, Fun2Work, which I created to offer services to companies and individuals who want help in bringing happiness into their lives, both professionally and personally. All the templates and downloads found in this book are available at www.Fun2Work.com/book-support/ in the Visitor section.

Disclaimer: Following the advice in this book could create happiness in your life and your immediate surroundings beyond your wildest dreams and completely transform your life. Also, the tools described here and at Fun2Work.com may help you attract things into your life that you have never imagined. So regardless of the claim I just made—the claims I made on the front cover, back cover, and throughout this book—I make no claims. Use at your own risk. Don't blame me or the publisher for anything bad that happens to you while trying to implement the advice in this book. If things should work out well for you, please write a long, five-star review on Amazon and blog weekly about how my book alone made a difference and transformed your life (like I said it would, by the way). Or if you feel like it, write to me at al@Fun2Work.com.

"The purpose of our lives is to be happy."

Dalai Lama

Introduction

HAPPINESS SEEMS SO COMPLEX AND hard to achieve that after seeking it for more than twenty-five years, I have decided to share some of my findings. Elusive for many and yet so obvious for a few, what is so magical about happiness that it is almost impossible to grasp and even harder to retain for any length of time?

In more than thirty years I have come across people who seemed to run around happily all day while others were always seeking happiness without even getting a glimpse. My fascination with happiness came in about the eighth year of my professional life when I started noticing that my customers were happy under a certain set of circumstances, as were my family, friends, and employees. Not only did they display happiness, they *exuded* happiness and made people around them happy also. What was the magic formula only a few seemed to possess? Being kind? Not at all, one of my first business encounters was with a very successful businessman named Bruno. He was the hardest and toughest man I had ever met, yet the people working for him seemed to be so happy—well, at least happier than most of my employees.

Looking back, it originally seemed incomprehensible and I found myself wondering how it could be possible that some people would be happy and a week later be unhappy under what seemed to be a similar set of circumstances. Multiple businesses and many employees later, it dawned on me that what seemed to be random situations were, in fact, a very precise set of behaviors that seemed to generate happiness around people.

For most of my life, I have been happy without really knowing why and how. At one point, I started wondering why some were happier than others and how they got to be so happy most of the time. It also appeared that money and status had nothing to do with how happy they were. I have to admit that I became obsessed with finding the source of happiness.

This book will answer the following question:
Where does happiness come from and how is it generated?

It is the will of this humble man to share with you a piece of my soul, and hopefully you will embark with me on the journey of creating happiness for yourself and everyone around you.

"Thousands of candles can be lighted from a single candle, and the life of the candle will not be shortened. Happiness never decreases by being shared."

Buddha

In Pursuit of Happiness

IT WAS APRIL 19, 2002 and I was sitting in my office alone. It had been seven years since I sold my company to Bartley Company, a large US competitor producing machinery for concrete products. Being alone at the office on a Friday evening was highly unusual for me, but then again, the entire evening was completely out of the ordinary.

Through the glass wall of my office, the darkness outside added to the sadness I felt deep down in my stomach, as it was my last day at the company that I'd helped build from the ground up. I got up and moved slowly toward the door, clumsily hitting the door frame on the way through. Though the pain was sharp, it didn't take anything away from the harsh feeling that had taken over my body. As I faced my assistant's office through the glass window, my heart tightened. It had been almost ten years since I'd hired Karen McDonald, a workaholic just as I was. Watching her go just minutes ago had been extremely difficult, but I'd asked her to leave so I would have a last moment alone with my first love.

Turning to the right and passing by the reception desk, I remembered that just a few hours earlier the receptionist had given me a big hug. In tears, we'd shared a brief moment together to conclude our twelve years of working together. I paused for a moment before making my way to the shop for the last time.

Through the hallway, which was barely lit with emergency lighting, I headed down the stairwell that took me past the shop superintendent's office. My anxiety grew with each step as I approached the shop door, where I hesitated for a moment, as I wasn't sure that I wanted it to be for the last time. Opening the door, I moved forward and stopped between two gigantic CNC machining centers. Surrounded by machines of all types and sizes in the shop, I felt at home. My heart was pounding as I took a deep breath and a last look around. Just as my lungs filled with air, sadness hit me like a ton of bricks. I teared up and then paused for what felt like an eternity, as I stood immobile and looked around me at what my partner and I had built over the past eighteen years.

Tonight, I was going to leave the building for the last time as president. My head had decided it was time to change my career, but my heart was still part of the company and the people that had helped me build the powerhouse I was about to leave. I remained rooted to the spot as my mind flashed back through memories of fantastic moments, some harder than others, but all good times, such as buying the company's first computer and teaching the secretary WordPerfect and Lotus 1-2-3. I thought of how we'd grown from two machinists to forty. For the best part of an hour my head and my heart were torn, yet to me it felt like just a split second before the deafening silence was broken by the old mechanical alarm signaling the shop break. I was abruptly jolted back into the present, where I had made the decision to move on with my career.

It was time to go.

"It is in your moments of decision that your destiny is shaped."

Tony Robbins

I was so deeply moved that night that I couldn't imagine it at the time, but my new quest for happiness would lead to many more encounters that shaped both my professional and my personal life. I have been blessed to have met many great people who have given me the opportunity to grow and be happy.

The decision to leave Bartley was quite simple: The potential joy of creating a better environment elsewhere seemed much more attainable than trying to preserve the company's happiness culture, which was currently under attack by headquarters. Such an environment takes years to create and in matter of months a bad boss can destroy it.

It had already taken me two years to realize that I'd been putting off moving forward, mainly due to my relationships with my employees. I had been trying to make things better, but in the end, it had become unbearable. I vividly recall a phone call with the president during which I had asked him how much notice he would like to get, should I decide to leave. His answer was quick; "Twenty-four hours," which just confirmed that he didn't appreciate my contribution, nor our success as a business unit.

We had received an unexpected fax one day, stating that a five-percent pay cut would be applied to all employees next pay period. I didn't know it at the time, but the president of Bartley Company had realized that he couldn't get to me directly, but he could hurt me by attacking my employees. I resisted for months, but in the end, he was the president, and his decision would prevail. It was then that I put the "seek joy/avoid pain" ratio in motion. Once the math was clear, it was only a matter of time before I took action, and it was quick—within two weeks it was done.

I will not go in detail in this chapter about how we actually function in our basic human operating system. For now, know that when we feel something is not working and we decide to act on that feeling, there is a mental calculation that we have already gone through before we make and act on that decision.

After I'd decided to leave Bartley, the original plan was to spend three months at Experienza in Mexico, an immersion training operation that offered classes and lodging for people who wanted to learn Spanish in the least amount of time. It seemed perfect for me before I headed into a new opportunity.

It didn't turn out quite that way.

First I flew to Bartley headquarters, which is located in Alpena, Michigan. Alpena is on the west side of Lake Huron, in the middle of nowhere, so getting there is no easy feat.

I had called for a meeting with Jerry, the owner and chairman of Bartley Company, and Ken, the president. When I arrived at the office, I was directed to the board room. I looked around at the very majestic setting and through the window looking into Jerry

Parker's office, I could see a map of the world made with small concrete blocks of different colors.

Jerry had been waiting for me and made his way from his office to the board room. He was a tall gentleman, who had inherited the presidency some twenty years earlier and had now moved on to become chairman. On the other side of the boardroom was Ken's office (current CEO). It was a grand setting, and all knew that a meeting in the board room was serious.

I had many times tried to bring up the conflict that was brewing between Ken and me to no avail, so Jerry Parker knew the topic that was about to be discussed. Each time the subject had been broached, Jerry had sent me back to Ken, not wanting to interfere.

Jerry's and my conversation remained casual for a moment before Ken walked in. Unaware of what was about to unfold, Ken was very courteous and friendly, offering the usual "How is everything?"

Once the decision to move on is made, we feel much better and our lives tend to move in more positive directions. I was more than ever ready to change scenery. I figured that the quicker it was over with, the easier it would be. There was no need to drag this on, I was there to do one thing and that was to resign.

I surprised them both by telling them that my office was in order, that my personal effects had already been moved back to my home, and that my computer was sitting on my desk and completely free of any personal files. Jerry turned to me and quickly said that there were no conflicts that couldn't be resolved, to which I replied that I had reached out many times and his refusal to get involved had pushed me to make the decision to leave. The discomfort between Ken and me had continued to escalate with no resolution in sight. I reiterated that Ken had asked for only twenty-four hours' notice, which was an obvious sign that he did not at all appreciate or respect my contribution, despite the fact that I had led my division to beat every ratio in the history of Bartley Company.

Jerry interjected, speaking of the past seven years we had worked together and in an attempt to get me to reconsider, he suggested that he would accept anything I asked for. After letting Jerry speak for a few minutes, I quickly offered that I would let him decide how long the notice period would be. Being a very candid and witty person, Jerry immediately shouted, "Ten years!" We all laughed for a moment and then I asked Jerry if he planned to keep Ken as president, to which he answered "Yes," without hesitation.

I then replied, "Three months." I told them I would cancel my trip to Mexico to make sure the transition would be smooth and that within a week, I would submit two candidates that I felt were ready to take my place.

Strangely enough, from then on Ken became much more friendly. I had always wondered if he had made my life miserable because he wanted me to leave. When he had taken over the presidency he had learned of the salary that I'd negotiated at the time I sold the company and I surmised that he thought I was making too much money. After all, we did have a very productive and profitable operation and we were all having fun in the process. The owners had publicly acknowledged many times that we were beating all records and that Ken should look into it. In most environments, having fun is synonymous with not working, but in my world, it is a sign of cooperation, productivity, and trust.

It didn't really matter—once I'd made the decision to move on, the past became irrelevant.

I headed back home and I ensured a smooth transition with the leadership team as well as with all the employees.

On my last day, upon arriving to the office, I walked up the stairs and made it to the reception desk where I was surprised to see everyone crammed into the office lunch room. To see the office staff would have been strange enough, but the shop people were also there waiting for me to arrive. They greeted me with such warmth, especially my assistant, Karen, who gave me a hug. It hit me then that it was the end of that road.

The moment arrived when Karen and Rene, the future GM, presented me with a rather large framed photo with an engraved plaque that read, "Nothing great is achieved without passion. Thank you for twenty years of passionate leadership." The photo showed the whole team standing on and in front of the last CNC machine we had purchased. A shop employee later told me that they had paid personally for the photographer and had insisted on not being paid during the photo shoot. I was not expecting that, and it touched me deeply.

Everyone who knows me would tell you that I never run out of words, but at that moment, I was speechless. My eyes teared up, my stomach turned mushy, and for a moment I was sinking into a trance. I was saved by my faithful assistant. Seeing that I was in trouble, Karen let go of the frame, took me in her arms, and gave me the biggest hug ever. It seemed to last over a minute, and it gave me enough time to regain my composure and face the rest of the crew, who were waiting to shake my hand and wish me well.

The burst of happiness that I experienced at that moment is hard to describe. I felt love and appreciation from all the employees present. At the same time, the commitment from all the employees who had personally paid for the frame made it all extremely overwhelming. The ultimate joy is felt at moments like these—when our expectations are surpassed far more than we could have ever expected.

Again, my decision to leave Bartley was purely a mathematical calculation of the pain felt when dealing with the president and the absence of joy on the job. Having said that, leaving for what was a very small company at the time, with a forty-percent pay cut might not seem an obvious choice to most…especially to my wife.

But when we have done the math and the decision is clear, our minds are at ease with whatever choice we are about to make or action we intend to take.

I walked in on my first day at Techniseal unsure of what I had signed up for. Surprisingly enough, everyone was happy to see me walk in the door on that Monday morning of May 6th, 2002. The previous president had been demoted a week earlier and everyone knows when you change the president, many other changes will follow.

All were waiting and seemed, in fact, relieved. As I turned to the right past the receptionist's desk, a young woman greeted me, and then the rest of the staff just lined up down the hall waiting to wish me well—most of them thinking that I was unknowingly entering Hell.

It took me nearly three months to assess the situation and come up with an executable plan to turn around this struggling organization. From the receptionist to the shipper, they were all in a constant state of disarray, not knowing if the boss would praise or complain on any given day. Furthermore, what was really strange was that though the management style was very laid back, when something came up, all hell broke loose and most employees sought cover wherever they could hide.

It is not uncommon to see small businesses that lack direction and funding being faced with this type of dynamic. Unfortunately, in these situations, it is almost impossible to retain good people. The instability creates such an unpleasant and unpredictable environment, that anyone who can find alternate employment, usually does.

One of my favorite sayings has always been: "It is not hard to retain non-productive people, they just won't go away on their own."

The hardest thing in a small business is to retain good people, especially because it is difficult to offer competitive salaries and great benefits when you can barely make ends meet. The challenges a small company faces are multiple, and some are lethal due to lack of funding. The only way to offset lack of security, great pay, and benefits is to make it worthwhile by becoming an organization that offers excitement and happiness.

The company had been growing slowly, but making little to no profit. The staff were always wondering if they would even have a job the following quarter. It took a few weeks for me to understand that the change in presidents was welcomed by most. There is very little possibility of happiness when our livelihood is uncertain; our survival instinct is on alert most of the time and it just ruins the morale and whatever joy can be found in the work.

In the following chapters I will share with you my own journey to happiness and introduce you to some of the tools I used in the process. I will explore how we operate at our most basic level and discuss how a decision as important as leaving my job at Bartley and jumping into a completely new venture, turned out to be one of the best decisions I ever made. In doing so, my wish is for you to get a glimpse of my process and shed some light on my pathway to happiness.

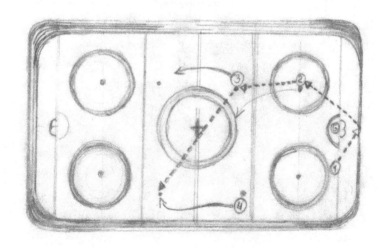

"Most people consider life a battle, though it's a game."

Florence Scovel Shinn

Life Is a Game

I WAS LUCKY ENOUGH TO have been born into an entrepreneurial family where early on, my parents taught us to understand cause and effect. At a very young age, I was taught that bad behavior would make it harder when pleading to get any favors; hence the basics of how life works.

As we grow up and get into our teenage years, the changes we go through often cause our memories to fail us, and when my father passed away, I did forget many of his teachings…temporarily.

My father's passing was brutal for me. I had just turned fifteen and I thought, like most teenagers, that I knew everything there is to know about life. My parents had put a lot of effort into teaching us the rudiments of life; simply put, how the game of life worked. But as I said, with the hormonal changes combined with my father's passing, my brain went AWOL. I did lose my mind for a while. When the light came back on, it became clear: There are a multitude of rules. Some are more explicit than others and there are some that are unwritten, but in the end, life becomes much smoother as we learn the rules. Of course there are opportunities, rules, and guidelines to navigate the game, but in essence, we are the captains of our lives and we need to choose the path to reach our ultimate destination.

This book will provide a toolset to play the game. Each chapter will elaborate on different tools to be used or considered during the process. Which situation we are facing at any particular time will greatly dictate which tool to employ. Some tools will appear to be simpler than others, and in the end, mastering them will help us navigate the game. Not all the tools need to be used at the same time and some may not be required at all. Some people will find Karma to be very useful, whereas others will find laws of attraction to be their pillar. Understanding how we think and make decisions will enable us to find our way through the maze. Keeping in mind that where we are has little bearing on where we are going, we will examine how we can ultimately reprogram our subconscious minds and redirect our destinations. In the latter part of the book, we will thoroughly examine the purpose of our lives and the effect this has on happiness and gratitude.

The game spans over a lifetime. We will be faced with situations that will feel odd sometimes, and feel loved, hated, and even miserable, but in the end, focusing on the toolset in this book will help us break through the fog and steer clear to our ultimate destination. It is up to the captain (you) to choose the tool that is more suited for your journey.

Happiness cannot be sustained without understanding the rules of the game. Learn the rules to maximize the fun part of your life... happiness.

As we become acquainted with the game, our level of happiness becomes more predictable. In other words, we become better players/planners, and planning in navigating our lives creates the solid ground to create a happiness-promoting environment.

As I navigated through life and reflected on the source of happiness, it became clear that we all had to abide by the rules of the game to win.

Every race and even species gains enormous momentum by acting as a social group. When facing any sort of challenge or aggression, there are huge advantages in acting with others in a coordinated fashion. The human race has taken control of the planet, and it is undeniable that one of the reasons we have progressed so far compared to other species is our superior ability to cooperate and act as a unified group.

Some races of monkeys and other mammals act in groups; monkeys and wolves hunt in a coordinated fashion and achieve much better results than if they tried to hunt on their own; birds fly in patterns, which makes long journeys more efficient; cyclists use the same strategy of replacing the leader to cut the wind for the followers. There are countless examples of cooperation in wildlife that yield synergies, but none equal the power humans have developed.

The evolution of the human race developed what could be referred to as "cooperation with recognition." Robert Cialvini calls it "reciprocating behavior." The human race is the only species that seems to have perfected this behavior and the result has been felt on a whole new level. The human race, for better or worse, now dominates the earth. Over time, as the ability to communicate improved, opportunities to cooperate increased, and the reciprocating behavior increased the ability of any group to overcome challenges by using credit for past deeds.

In order for a group to function efficiently together, there need to be rules; rules, conventions, or guiding principles of the group. Rules and guidelines follow us all our lives, unless we happen to live in a cabin in a wooded area where no one else wants to venture. For the purpose of these writings we will stick to normal societal rules. Spiritual rules exist as well, but these rules will not be covered in this book since they are of a very personal nature and are covered elsewhere by much better authorities on the subject.

Once our ancestors decided to operate in groups or societies, each group operated under rules passed down from generation to generation. The rules must be followed to ensure the wellbeing of a group. In the span of a lifetime, everyone will be subjected to many different sets of rules. To better illustrate this, we can refer to federal, state, municipal, school, and household regulations. They are all of different competences and they will at one time or another influence our lives; present and future. If we understand the rules we should succeed relatively well in life—if we oppose them, we may have a rougher ride.

We are initially exposed to household rules, and then when we start school or kindergarten we quickly find that another layer of rules is suddenly pushed upon us. As we continue to grow up, more layers of rules and regulations will be added, and it becomes more and more confusing, especially if our parents haven't prepared us to some extent for the way society operates. Since our parents, and their parents before them agreed to operate within a society, there are certain rules that must be followed to ensure our wellbeing as well as that of others around us. This book will not delve into a philosophical debate on whose society is better but will focus on happiness. You may be surprised to learn that the society in which we live has very little bearing on how happy we are or will be.

When we realize that life is a game and we must understand the rules, it becomes easier to move ahead with whatever we decide to undertake. There are levels of games that can be played and choosing the right level will give the appropriate amount of joy. As an example, in school we may simply want to study and move on to the next grade without making too many waves, while others may want to be class representative or join student activities in a leadership role. This constitutes a level up in the school game. As we grow up there are also different levels of gaming we can engage in, or we can decide to keep it at the basic level and go with the flow. There are also many levels in the workplace, and as we decide to step up our game, the game gets harder and needs more understanding and finesse. The foundations that we have, the ways in which we were raised, the experiences we had as children, and our schooling all enable us, to some degree, to access higher levels in the game. Playing the game at a high level can be exhilarating for some and debilitating for others so it is critical to choose wisely. When we choose to push and stretch ourselves to the limit of our capabilities, we will maximize our growth potential. But be cautious at this point—the more we push the limit, the higher the reward, but so is the risk. As long as we keep this risk/reward equation in check, we should be mentally safe.

Motivation is undeniably the factor that will help us justify the effort needed to understand the game and play it well. When parents fail to teach basic rules to their kids, sooner or later the children will be exposed to the system (THE GAME) and the awakening may be brutal. When exposed to the set of rules, depending on how we were raised as children, there are several possible ways in which we will react; acceptance, comprehension, or rebellion. It is pretty simple to predict where this is heading—the kids who were taught early on to understand the rules and make the best of it will, in general, perform better in most situations from childhood to adulthood. The ones who were forced into acceptance will get along. Most of them will do fairly well because they were taught to go with the flow and they will usually end up getting a fair shake from society. The kids who were not taught how to deal with the rules of the game usually end up in trouble. There is a side note that needs to be made here. Not all rebels end up in trouble and not all accepting kids get a fair or bad shake, nor do the gamers all get great lives. In general, though, we will find that these three types of kids will end up in their respective categories.

The game has rules and we must learn how to navigate inside the system. It is no different than playing Monopoly with our friends and family. The sooner we learn the rules, the better we will get at the game. Life works the same way. When we are young, the other players of a game will give us some leeway, but as we get to know the rules, they will more or less assume we know the game and will not tolerate any deviations from the rules. If we do not respect the rules, they will notify us and at one point they will punish us for not following the rules and will likely not want us to play in their game. Life functions this way as well. There are layers and layers of rules that should have been learned as we grew up—the best gamers were coached early. I personally find it strange that we don't seem to have any interest in teaching the fundamentals of how life works in school. It is left to the parents and I believe that some are really great at it while others are absolutely not. Probably the old saying that goes something like this applies: "You can't give what you don't have." Parents who have not been taught how to play the game will most likely not be able to help their kids in that respect.

Although my short stay in the military taught me a lot about rules and how to navigate, once I got out of university, I took life way too seriously. It was like I had forgotten the lessons learned in the armed forces, and until I woke up and paid the price, I struggled way too much for the results I got. It is far more enjoyable to play with players who love the game and play it well. People who take life too seriously will inevitably generate unnecessary frustrations... which I did cause early in my career and in my family life.

Once we understand that the ultimate goal of the game is to maximize our happiness, a lot of what we live through starts to make sense. Picture yourself entering the game. You need to become an astute player and you, and only you, know what makes you happy. In fact, no one has ever made another person happy.

There are three major factors to consider entering the game. First, we are all part of a game; second, the ultimate goal of our lives is happiness; and third, we are the captains of our lives and choose our own paths to our destinations.

Finding a mentor is a simple way to help us understand the game better. Usually we will find that most successful people show certain common traits and values. In the following paragraphs I have listed some of my favorite guidelines and values.

Life is a game. Understand the rules and enjoy the game... your LIFE.

I love the simple way of living explained in Don Miguel Ruiz's book, *The Four Agreements:*

The Four Agreements

1. BE IMPECCABLE WITH YOUR WORD
   a. Speak with integrity.
   b. Say only what you mean.
   c. Never use words to gossip about others.
   d. Use the power of words to promote love and appreciation.

2. DON'T TAKE ANYTHING PERSONALLY
   a. What others do belongs to them.
   b. Others' actions are a projection of their own reality.
   c. Others act on their beliefs, you shouldn't live their reality.

3. DON'T MAKE ASSUMPTIONS
   a. Ask questions and express what you want.
   b. Eliminating ambiguity will help everyone around you.

4. ALWAYS DO YOUR BEST
   a. Always do your best, no matter what the circumstances are.
   b. When you have done your best, you will feel free from regret or self-judgement.

In a more general sense, these agreements, which we make with ourselves, will help us through the game. Sometimes we will be faced with decisions that are not always clear-cut and the four agreements are a basic compass that makes decision-making much simpler.

Exercise:
List a few examples where you applied the four agreements and where you have ignored them, then reflect on the outcome of each situation. There is no better way to illustrate this effect of the game on our lives.

By no means do I consider that I have a perfect life, but for the most part I have tried to navigate my life with these guidelines in mind... most of the time.

"Treat other people with the concern and kindness you would like them to show toward you." This saying has come to be called the Golden Rule.

"Do unto others as you would have them do unto you," is a commandment based on the words of Jesus in the Sermon on the Mount:

"All things whatsoever ye would that men should do to you, do ye even so to them."

I hope these guidelines and rules will help you as much as they have helped me navigate through my life. It is not enough to create an outer framework to promote the creation of happiness. Within that framework we need to instill habits that support us and help us move toward our primary goal...happiness.

> *"Do not take life too seriously.*
> *You will never get out of it alive."*
>
> Elbert Hubbard

SUMMARY

Life is a game and there are the players who learn the game and the ones who just go along. The people who fail to understand the basic concept of our society and don't learn to work within the rules of the game will have a tougher time. Understanding that we are the captains of our lives is crucial in taking responsibility for the paths we will take during our journeys through the game. And finally, while acknowledging that happiness is our ultimate goal, mastering the tools laid out in this book will help us achieve our ultimate destination... happiness.

"Karma has no menu, you get served what you deserve."

Anonymous

Karma

AS I'VE GONE THROUGH LIFE, I have looked for patterns and often asked successful people how they manage business, life, and mostly family.

Patterns are relevant because history repeats itself.

One of the patterns that I observed early on is that most very successful people are kind. I did wonder if kindness was the result of being successful or the other way around. It turned out that being kind was my way to success, and I would like you to get a first-hand look at a phenomenon that seems to intrinsically tally your kindness or lack thereof.

Karma is a strange phenomenon—some believe it while others ignore its existence. In the end it is a matter of choice. There are many laws in this world that we ignore and Karma is an easy one to overlook.

There are laws such as the law of gravity, which we learn very early. When a child drops something on his foot once or twice, even at a young age he realizes that there is something pulling stuff downward. Karma is a lot more subtle, making it easy to ignore.

I have always envisioned Karma a bit like a slot machine, with the exception that we can put negative credits in the Karma bank as well as positive credits.

There are some people who spend their time at casinos hoping to leave with lots more money than they came with. Some do win big, but there are very few of them compared to the number of people who make deposits in the casino bank and walk away with nothing. The gambler-type might be willing to ignore Karma. It is a choice and there is no hard proof that Karma exists, making it easy for many to pretend it doesn't exist. I always thought that it was too great a risk to ignore it.

Let's imagine a bank where we could accumulate all our good deeds and of course the not-so-great ones. We do not control the withdrawal process, which seems to operate on its own and at random. Having said that, when I take the time to look closer at my everyday life, there are some outstanding coincidental happenings that seem so natural they are simply making my life just a tad easier on a regular basis.

Some people believe in Karma. I am one of those and I have lived my life accordingly. When in doubt, I have always given more than most, helped more than most thought needed, and expected nothing in return. It turns out that the universe always gives it back to me, many times over.

I love the phrase, "The harder you work, the luckier you get." This has turned out to be true over and over again in my life. The harder I work, the more opportunities show up. Is it truly a coincidence? Is it Karma? Or is it the result of a sequence of events? When we work hard or help others there are thoughts that are conveyed by the people we work with or help. These people speak highly of us since they feel our actions to be positive towards them. Not surprisingly, they will subsequently use thoughts, words, and actions that will most likely put into motion a situation with the potential to be beneficial to us in the future.

When we are kind to others, kind people will show up in our lives. It is a fact that nice people hang around nice people. Putting it simply, we are, in fact, creating the response first in our heads and then expressing it in words. It will then be reflected in our actions and ultimately in the response of our immediate environment. That phenomenon is truly a wonderful system that will eventually pay us back. The energy we exude will attract people who have the same energy. When you see someone who is always complaining, look around and you will notice that most people surrounding that individual will also eventually complain, if they are not already doing so. People want to keep company with people who live on the same energy level.

> "Everything is energy and that's all there is to it.
> Match the frequency of the reality you want and you
> cannot help but get that reality. It can be no other way.
> This is not philosophy. This is physics."
>
> Albert Einstein

All throughout my life I have helped others. Often, the people around me would wonder why I bothered to take the time. During our early stages together, my wife would often ask why…"Why would you help [this guy or that one]? He will never help you back."

> "Actions are the seed of fate, deeds grow into destiny."
>
> Harry S. Truman

I studied at Montreal University and lived on campus in a huge twin-tower residence. On the first floor there was a café where a beautiful young lady worked. Each day, she would smile at everyone, but I could not get her attention other than being served coffee with her beautiful smile every time. She was very athletic and was five years younger than I was. She ran every day and swam almost every week to stay fit.

I have never been the type to run, but one day when she was looking for a walking partner to run errands in town, I volunteered without hesitation, thinking it was the greatest opportunity available to get to know her more than casually at the café.

We took the short road to the main street, which consisted of going down the rather long stairs in front of Montreal University. As we were going down the stairs, we crossed paths with an elderly couple, who were probably attending a summer immersion session and staying at the university residence. The couple had just made it onto the landing midway up and were gasping for air, obviously struggling from hauling their luggage up the stairs. I hesitated for a moment because I was chasing that beautiful woman I was with and did not want to detract from my prime mission, (which seemed to be going a whole lot better than it had been in the past months). I looked at my companion for a moment, gave her a smile, and then ran both sets of luggage to the top of the stairs before running back down to the landing. The couple were still resting and thanking the girl I was with for sending me up with their luggage. The relief and smiles on their faces were priceless, but I was surprised that my companion was getting the credit for something she had not been part of. To this day my wife remembers this action, and I truly believe that it was one of the reasons she saw firsthand the good in me, or at least it was a contributing factor that helped me convince her to start dating me.

It doesn't matter what we do nor does it matter who we do it for, Karma is an accumulator that will pay us back when time comes. Some people play slot machines every weekend in the hope that the machine will pay back and give them a portion of someone else's money so they can go home with winnings. Unlike gambling, Karma doesn't require other people to lose for you to win. It is a choice to trust in Karma and every time I do a good deed, I am convinced that it goes straight into my Karma bank.

> *"As you sow, so shall you reap."*
>
> King James' Bible, Epistle to the Galatians, 6:7

Karma is a funny force. No one has a precise grasp on how it works or what triggers it, but at the time of this writing, I am in my late fifties and I am living proof that Karma is a force to be reckoned with.

I'm always fascinated whenever I've met people from my childhood who've said I was lucky that I had inherited my father's business genes. Unfortunately, my father passed away when I was just fifteen years old. The genes may have helped, but the little time I was lucky enough to have with him planted the seed that would eventually bring me to where I am today. I will go into this in the last chapter of this book. For now, though, let me say I do feel lucky if I have inherited my father's business genes, but I also believe that I worked hard every step of the way and that the success I enjoy today is because I get back what I put in—Karma.

There are a few things that I have done in the past that I am not proud of, especially during the period that I revolted after my father's passing, but I have regretted every single occurrence, and for the most part, I have done no harm to anyone nor wished anyone ill.

My life turned around after a good friend of mine was shot and killed. He was working as the doorman of a strip club and unfortunately dealt drugs on the side. One evening a deal turned bad and he took six bullets. That triggered an instant rage in his brother, Gaby, and me. In the hope of getting revenge, we set out together to find out who had done this. We did get quite close; one month later, Gaby was shot and left for dead by a stranger coming out of a bar. Luckily, he survived, although he had to spend over a month in the hospital. I believe that he survived because he had done great things all his life. For me, it was the wakeup call I needed to get out of that lethargic state I had been in for the past four years.

Many brave people join the army to serve and help their country. I joined because I was scared to death and needed a place to hide. Not knowing what to do after hearing how my best friend had ended up in the hospital between life and death, I visited my godfather, who happened to be one of the most generous men I have ever known. In a blink he convinced me that my father's passing had left me with a lack of discipline and the army was the answer to all of my problems—fear being the least of them.

Today I strongly believe that my short stay in the military put me back on track and saved my life. Was it Karma? Luck? It was certainly one of those two.

I would like to end this chapter by sharing with you the twelve laws of Karma. I strongly believe that when observing these simple laws, our lives turn out much better. I hope for you that they will bring as much love and happiness into your life as they did mine.

The twelve laws of Karma can guide us to achieve the life that we desire:

1. The Great Law
As you sow, so shall you reap, or the Law of Cause and Effect. What we put out into the Universe is what comes back to us.

2. The Law of Creation
We attract what we are, not what we want. To get the life we want, we have to actively create it rather than just waiting for it to happen.

3. The Law of Humility
To grow, we must accept what is, rather than arguing that it shouldn't be. To reach a higher state, we have to stop judging and accept life, while still taking action to make the world a better place.

4. The Law of Growth
The only way to change the world is to change ourselves. It is we who must change, not the people around us. When we change who and what we are within our hearts our lives begin to change too.

5. The Law of Responsibility
When there is turbulence in one's own life, there is often turbulence internally. If we're to change our lives, we must change our frames of mind and surroundings.

6. The Law of Connection
Everything in the Universe is connected. Each step leads to the next step and one is not more important than another.

7. The Law of Focus

You cannot think of two things at the same time. If we focus on higher values, lower thoughts like anger or greed cannot enter.

8. The Law of Giving

If one believes something to be true, then sometime in their life they will be called upon to demonstrate that truth. Here is where one puts what they *claim* to have learned into *practice*.

9. The Law of Here and Now

If we live in the past or the future, we are unable to take action in the only moment we truly control, which is *now*.

10. The Law of Change

History repeats itself until we learn the lessons that we need to learn in order to move forward. We must accept the past and learn its lessons.

11. The Law of Patience and Reward

We must consistently take action towards creating the life that we want. In the end, doing work we love that is meaningful to us is its own reward.

12. The Law of Significance and Inspiration

You get back from something whatever you have put into it. The true value of something is equal to the energy and intent that is put into it.

If we follow these laws of Karma, we can be assured that our contribution to the world will be a positive one. We will also reap the rewards of peace, love, and happiness in our own lives.

> SUMMARY
> Karma is very high on my list. It is easy to overlook, but I believe that it is a big mistake to ignore it.
> Karma is like a bank—we store good and bad credits. In the end, we will get served what we deserve.

"The aim of the wise is not to secure pleasure, but to avoid pain."

Aristotle

Seek Joy/Avoid Pain

I HAVE CHASED HAPPINESS ALL my life and for the longest time, I did not have the experience or the toolset to achieve it, or even the understanding of why happiness seemed so random. We all have moments of enlightenment; it need not be to the magnitude of Einstein's theory of relativity. Want it or not, we negotiate all our lives, starting when we are babies crying to get our parents' attention, to when we negotiate with our kids who want to put us in a retirement home. It is the essence of what we go through in our lives.

Through the years, I noticed that I possessed a gift…negotiation. At first, it seemed that I had it naturally, but after a while, it became clear that there was a method behind my success in negotiation. Not only was I good at it, most of the time both parties left the table happy.

Negotiation is an art form and the people who get what they want by way of negotiation in an open and direct way are superstars. It is important to distinguish them from the bullies who use their position, title, size, or other means of intimidation to get what they want.

Now, having said the above, I must point out that the astute negotiator takes the time to understand what would make the other party happy, while not losing focus on the primary goal, which is getting what he wants.

Understanding what the other side wants is the cornerstone of negotiation, and how people decide what they want is the key to the whole process.

What I thought to be a gift happens to simply be an understanding of how most of us evaluate all situations we are facing, which is how we make one decision rather than another one.

After years of chasing the "How, What, and Why," here it is: All species operate with the same modus operandi: Seek joy/avoid pain.

Like most people, I hadn't reflected on the decision process most people use to choose whatever action or decision they make.

In recent years, however, in the quest for happiness, I did take the time to put a lot of thought into it, and it is really quite revealing. As awkward as it may seem, the process is a very simple one, almost too simple to be true.

It appears that when something seems simple, it doesn't resonate true in our minds, hence the expression, "It's too good to be true." When something appears to be too simple, we set out to find what is complicated about it. That may be the reason we tend to over-complicate everything. Nonetheless, I am a true believer that simplicity is present in most of our lives and that taking a look with the simplicity lens may help us better understand how we make most of our decisions.

Joy and pain are closely related, in fact they are both on the same continuum. Imagine a line that starts on the left as very painful while one to the far right is very pleasant (see Fig. 1). Somewhere close to the middle there is a zone of indifference in which most of us are comfortable. What is really important to note is that the indifference zone is not the same for everyone. For some people, it is a very fine line, whereas for others the zone can be very wide. It all depends on our individual tolerance level. Furthermore, depending on our individual tolerance level, we may be willing to sustain a certain amount of pain even before considering that it is uncomfortable.

Fig. 1

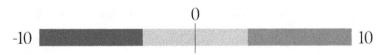

At first glance it is not obvious that the decisions we make greatly influence our happiness, or the potential for happiness. Understanding what motivates most of our decisions may at some point help us understand how to plan our happiness or at least to understand why we make the decisions that keep us from being happy.

Most species automatically operate under the same modus operandi: Seek joy and avoid pain. For a virus, joy/pain will be survival/death. A simple way to illustrate this is that the virus will mutate and move to a nearby host in an attempt to multiply and survive. A dog will do tricks to get our attention and stop certain behaviors to prevent being punished.

I believe that most often, people are happiness-seeking beings. By that I mean that whatever thoughts we have and actions we take are oriented, for the most part, toward what we believe at the time will provide us with the most joy and/or the least pain.

We seek joy in all actions and decisions we make and when we make these decisions, we assess the risk of pain in our actions. When the sum of potential short-term and long-term joy clearly exceeds the risk of potential pain, we move in that direction without much further thought or consideration.

	Status Quo		Alternative
Scenario A	$Joy_1 - Pain_1$ **When you leave your relationship**	<	$Joy_2 - Pain_2 - Pain_{Leaving}$
Scenario B	$Joy_1 - Pain_1$ When you stay in your relationship	>	$Joy_2 - Pain_2 - Pain_{Leaving}$ If pain of leaving is much greater than Scenario A

A person considering leaving their present employment; Scenario A, would evaluate the total joy felt at the present employment minus the pain. When the pain exceeds the joy, usually alternate employment is considered. When considering leaving the employment, the expected joy minus the expected pain will be evaluated and the pain of leaving will also be part of the equation (Alternative).

In our example above, the employee may like the present job, but the boss is nasty and very unpleasant, which together, leaves the employee with a negative feeling (Status Quo).

When contemplating an alternate employment, the employee will consider changing only if the prospective employment offers a positive joy vs pain feeling. But before changing, he will also consider the pain of changing; factors like friends on the job, proximity to one's home, and possibly the spouse's opinion on the new opportunity. The new opportunity is placed in the formula. If Status Quo offers less joy than the Alternative, usually the individual will accept the new opportunity.

On the other hand, if the pain of leaving, combined with the joy minus the pain of the new opportunity, is negative compared to Status Quo, then the employee will most likely remain in his current job (Scenario B).

I have used an employment scenario, but this formula applies to all our situations; for example being in a partnership, a friendship, or a marriage. A marriage is a bit more complicated if kids are part of the equation, since the pain of leaving takes into account many more aspects, such as the pain inflicted directly on the kids, the rest of the family's perception, etc.

When Bill Gates or Warren Buffet give 100M$ to a charity, they proceed with the same modus operandi. Is it truly the joy from seeing the good the money will give to others, or is it the fact that it will make them look good all over the news? In either case, the joy anyone gets from an action is very personal and cannot be contemplated easily by others, but no one gives any amount of money to charity if they do not get joy out of it. Keep in mind that giving 100M$ has much less of an effect on Warren's or Bill's standard of living than most of us giving 100$; something many people do several times a year and never make the news.

> *"Folks are usually about as happy
> as they make their minds up to be."*
>
> Abraham Lincoln

There are a myriad of professionals who make a living out of trying to get us to believe that life in its basic form is complex. The society that we live in is making us believe that life is complicated. There is something about our era that makes our lives complicated or at least there is the perception that people cannot cope with their reality. They have fallen into the trap of this perception, subconsciously starting to believe that life is not as simple as it is in reality. When someone starts believing that their situation is out of hand, confusion ensues and they lose track of their reality.

To see a patient lying on a couch describing to a psychologist what makes their life so miserable may seem odd to some of us. The professional will try to get the patient back on track by making him realize on his own that what seems so big in his mind is, in reality, a trivial matter. At that point the patient usually starts to get better. Whenever we see reality for what it is and keep it in front of us for what it is really worth, we see that whatever problem we face is rarely insurmountable.

Some situations that are not under our control may create an enormous amount of pain, which left unattended, may cause very negative subconscious imprints.

Death of a loved one is a prime example. In the case of a long terminal illness, we can feel terrible pain, although we should be able to understand that our loved one may be much better off resting in peace rather than sticking around and suffering. In these cases, the services of a professional can provide a great deal of relief and support.

The same pain applies to sudden death by accident. Most other situations can be rationalized in simple terms.

Humans have complicated this simple concept and made it so that when things don't go our way some of us feel the need to consult with experts, who will dig into the source of our problems. Most psychologists will get us to talk through our issues; in essence, they will pull out the pain points until we realize that unless we are injured in an irreparable way, we may find a meaning to life after all, and hence get back to a positive joy/pain relationship or ratio.

Applying the joy/pain formula when analyzing what we are going through helps us in keeping the real issue in the forefront. I have met with many employees throughout my life, and our most productive discussions were always the ones where we were able to get down to the bottom of the issue. Almost inevitably it came down to a simple: "I like this, but that really bothers me—that is why my behavior has not been so productive." In other words, it rarely appears simple, but it is rarely very complicated. When we cut through all the clutter, it all comes down to a simple joy vs pain ratio, which again goes back to our basic programming. I will go into further detail on this, in the chapter "Our Brains and Computers."

On that note, our conscious, as well as our subconscious minds, can trigger a need to make a decision. Our family or friend may bring to our attention that we have a problem that needs attention, and the same model applies.

One day you come back from your garage, or simply step out of your car, and decide that you are better off getting a new car rather than constantly pumping money into the old clunker that has been paid-off for a while. You add up the repairs over the past year and factor in the risk of being stranded on the side of the road versus getting a new car or a more recent model…along with a new set of payments. You look at the mortgage on the house, private schooling for the kids, new bikes, family vacation, etc. and evaluate the risk of losing your job. Once these calculations are done, it becomes very easy to support a decision one way or another—but again, that is how we make even a small decision.

In our relationships, it is easy to understand why friends keep getting together or stop after a while. In the event that the perceived joy exceeds the pain of getting together on a regular basis, the routine encounters will continue. The reverse is also true, where if the pain exceeds the joy, the relationship will dwindle down slowly or maybe even come to a brutal stop.

Relationships with friends are usually simpler than marriages or relationships with life partners, but although they are more complex due to kids, houses, and common bank accounts, the same logic applies. Why do couples stay together? It is a simple joy minus pain calculation. When we add all the joy we get from a relationship and take away all the pain, when the result is positive the choice is clear and most couples will remain in the relationship. When it becomes unclear that staying in a relationship offers more joy than the perceived pain, the decision to leave is contemplated. On the other hand, when the perceived pain of leaving is greater, the decision to stay in a painful relationship is most often made.

Keep in mind while doing this exercise that there are far more variables that we take into account consciously and even subconsciously in a very subtle way in our heads and hearts. The potential pain that we may inflict on our children, our families, friends and other relationships, and the repercussions on them over time weigh heavily in the balance. In the end, the more we analyze, the more we weigh every aspect of the relationship and its positive or negative outcome, the clearer the choice will become.

"Life is really simple, but we insist on making it complicated."

Confucius

Understanding what motivates our thoughts and actions helps us steer through the clutter.

SUMMARY

The seek joy/avoid pain ratio is and will always be the deciding mechanism we use to decide on which option or action to take. It is as basic as it gets. When we slow down and reflect on our decision process, there is no other way. Humans and all animals use the same decision-making process: Seeking joy or avoiding pain is the most reliable predictor in any decision process.

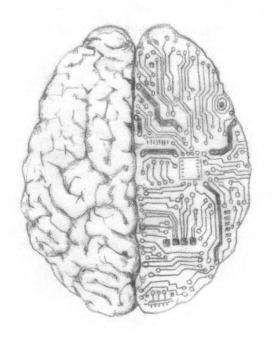

In terms of the brain, you can, in a crude way, think of the human brain as a computer."

Paul Greengard

Our Brains and Computers

THERE ARE MOMENTS IN OUR lives that define our futures. One of those happened during my first year at Bishop's University when a professor passed on an article that actually changed the course of my life. As an introduction to this chapter I have decided to include it, and it will also explain why after registering as business major, I developed a strong inclination towards computer science.

I hope you will enjoy the extract:

The following is a summary of the plot of a story, "The Last Question" written by Isaac Asimov in 1956. The summary appeared in *Psychology Today*; 2nd Edition, 1972.

> Mankind, thanks to its giant computers, has managed to work out systems for making use of solar energy, and it appears that a golden age will be dawning—free energy without pollution. One minor official, however, worries about what will happen when the sun runs down. Will mankind be able to wind it up again, so to speak? He asks the computer, which can only say it has insufficient data to give an answer.
>
> Over centuries and millennia men learn to travel between the stars and to colonize the galaxy. They learn the secret of immortality. They free themselves of their material bodies and become energy beings living in space. At every state they are helped by the information-analyzing ability of computers, which steadily grow more complex. Indeed, computers grow so complex that only computers themselves can design and construct still better computers. The result is that mankind loses all physical connection with the vast central computer that becomes the great problem solver in man's later history. At one stage, this computer occupies an entire world by itself. Then parts of it actually exist outside space. Finally, although all of it exists outside space, it still keeps itself at

the disposal of man. Any man can ask any question at any point in the universe and get an answer.

Through all of history, however, no matter how widespread and ethereally immortal men become, it is clear that the entire universe is running down. Available energy decreases, and the stars are dimming to final extinction. Periodically, someone asks the ever-improving computer if the universe can ever be wound up again. Always, the computer answers that it doesn't have enough information to formulate an answer. Finally, the end comes. The last stars are all but dead. Mankind has coalesced into one energy being that is pure mind, and at the last it coalesces with the ultimate computer that exists outside space. Now only the computer is left. And the computer cannot reset, for in all man's history there remains that one question it could not answer—the last question. Can one wind up the universe once more?

Ages pass while the computer endlessly analyzes all the information gathered in the course of a trillion years, and finally it has the answer. But now no one remains to tell it to, so the computer decides to answer the question in such a way that there will eventually be someone to understand. The computer began ...

And it said, "Let there be light!" And there was light! ...

WARNING:
In this chapter I may offend some people by making inferences about the human brain and its similarities with computers. It is not my intention to offend, but to clearly illustrate some concepts around the human brain, it is necessary to draw some parallels that may be disturbing for some.

I am also sure that I will take a beating from all sides; from the psychologists, the biologists, and the medical doctors, to the computer scientists. To give you the best of my knowledge and experience, I will proceed with its encumbrances from the experts.

This chapter may seem a bit long-winded, but we need to push through this mind-bending exercise to set the groundwork for the reader to grasp concepts that have been covered by many in too broad a sense to actually make sense. I will try to give it a layman's view in the hope of making it easier to understand. If you bear with me through this, I personally guarantee that it will be worth your time and make sense in the next chapter.

I would like you to take a leap of faith and come with me on a short journey into the realm of technology, science, and imagination for a moment. Having a background in management and computer science, I will try to set the groundwork in the coming paragraphs by explaining in the simplest possible way how computers work. I will then attempt to draw some similarities with our brains.

The large IBM super computers and the smart phones that are so popular today are very similar to the first Apple computer that Steve Wozniak and Steve Jobs built in Jobs' parents' garage in the mid-70s. Though they have evolved significantly in the last forty years, gaining speed and memory capacity, the basic components remain the same. A series of electronic relays, which have evolved to be semiconductors, deal with a binary sequence that enables the electronic parts to come alive and execute commands following the programming sequence. These programs were initially entered into the computer with switches, then cards, and eventually with magnetic tapes. The need to store more and more data led to floppy disks, then hard drives, and finally, high-storage dynamic and static memory chips. Hard drives are still the most widely used today.

When the power is turned on and components are energized, an initial chip is powered and its simple instruction is to load the Basic Input/Output System "BIOS" into live memory. This set of instructions tells the computer how to deal with all of its components. The next instruction will be to load the Operating System "OS." These commands will enable the hardware to execute a given set of instructions called a *program,* or in the case of a smart phone, an *app,* which can be called up by the user or operator, depending on the task to be executed.

In this day and age, we may not even be aware that the BIOS is booting up our computers because the computing power has become so great that the screen shows a nice scene or a moving circle. It then automatically calls the Windows Operating System in the case of a PC, or on a Mac, it will call MAC OS X or any of its predecessors. Keep in mind that components need energy to get into motion. We will track back to energy later on. The computer has a few more components that also resemble the human brain: Random Access Memory (RAM), which to our brain would be our short-term memory, and a hard drive, which would be comparable to our long-term memory. For now, suffice to say that there is a close relationship between a computer's components and the human brain.

Since we have been trying to get a computer to execute human tasks, it is only natural that we have been trying to emulate the brain's functions in many respects.

Having said all the above and hopefully not having lost too many readers in the process, let's draw some more parallels with our brains.

From the moment we are conceived until we die, our brains have at their cores a basic code that enables the fetus to develop and grow into an adult. We refer to this as DNA and it includes all the instructions needed to grow and develop into an adult as well as instructions on how to interact with all of our sensory organs and other systems that we don't really control, such as our hearts, lungs, our hormone secretion systems, and regulation, along with a myriad of other functions that would be too long to enumerate.

Our basic instructions are much more complex than a computer's operating system, but in essence they are closely related.

Most scientists who have studied DNA agree that it is a code that lays the foundation on how our bodies will develop in time. DNA is a string of instructions that have a very close relationship to computer programming code. We still do not understand all of the DNA code, but in recent years we have been making significant progress that enables us to state that DNA determines much of our physical and mental attributes.

Computer development has advanced so much that it now has reached a state that enables self-diagnostics. This is the first step in being able to fix oneself. Computers are getting more sophisticated and powerful as their operating systems evolve and continue to get much more complex. Until recently, programming had to be done by humans, however, in recent years we have written programs that enable computers to write program for themselves—in essence, self-programming. This concept is important as we will discuss how we can also reprogram ourselves to a certain level for better or worse.

You may wonder why I am taking you through all this computer jargon. There are similarities I want to highlight. As a computer user you can influence the computer's method of navigating its programming by making selections when prompted. In the case of humans, we can consciously control our breathing and to some extent how quickly or slowly our hearts beat. We also control how we think and interact with others.

We do control our thoughts, but if we analyze closely, we will find that the first reaction to most interactions is influenced by our subconscious. Suffice to say that we need to be more conscious of this background programming.

Today we have reached the stage that components and memory speed are opening the way to enable programmers as well as computers themselves, i.e. Artificial Intelligence, to mimic the human brain.

Today's modern components mimic the human brain and actually modify the program code to enable the computer to learn. We refer to this as Artificial Intelligence, "AI." As for humans, we spend our entire lives learning. Some of us are more stubborn than others, but most of us will accumulate knowledge until we die. In turn, this learning function enables us to alter our ways of thinking, in essence the way we perceive things. Our internal programming, mostly subconscious, is constantly monitoring our thoughts, as well as what we say and do. This is a critical concept to keep in mind as we navigate to how we can affect our internal program.

As of today, a computer cannot change its BIOS (basic input/output system). It is still a chip that is embedded in the hard circuitry of the computer. Luckily for humans, we have such a basic operating system that when we lose consciousness, the basic operating system will keep our vital functions going even though we are not conscious. We cannot alter our basic operating system either, at least to the best of my knowledge.

Computers are now capable of changing their programming as they go. We can also change our programs as time goes by and I will give a description of this process in the next chapter. Both computers and human beings run on energy—without energy, neither would be able to function for any given amount of time.

To the best of my knowledge, in all the mighty power of energy, there are only three types of energy that we truly control in this world. These are thoughts, words, and actions. Everything else is accessory to our actions.

Energy is an unbelievably complex phenomenon, and at its core there appears to be a grand connection between all of its components. Since nothing can grow without energy, it would be naive to think that there is no common connection with nature and our surroundings. At first glance it appears that there are multiple sources of energy when we look far away—there are other sources of energy, which may lead to the philosophical debate of "Are we the only ones?" For now, I will stay away from this debate and focus on our essential source of energy: the sun. Without the sun, most scientists agree that life would not exist on Earth. With millions of years of evolution and grace from the sun's energy, the planet and its habitants have grown and evolved into what we are today. We have created computers in our image, and the more computers evolve, the more their programming becomes complex and they are able to perform tasks too complex for humans.

As computer knowledge advances and complex programming improves, we are beginning to see more and more Artificial Intelligence (AI). The development of AI, which today is at the forefront of technology, enables us to open our minds to the extent computers are becoming increasingly complex and powerful.

We have been told by doctors and psychologists that the human brain is complex, and it definitely is. The programming of our operating system, however, is a lot less complex. Our conscious mind operates in a very binary way in the way we think. We can only process one set of data at a time, and unlike massive computers, we have a single processor and deal with one issue at a time. For a number of years, I was one of many people who thought that multi-tasking was a very efficient way of doing two or more tasks at once. I recently found out differently. My daughter works as a recruiter at a well-known firm and recently attended a workshop in which the presenter ran the audience through an exercise that I would like to share with you.

This simple exercise will clearly show that multi-tasking is not as effective as we would like to think. For the exercise, use a stop watch, the timer on your smart phone, or any other device that enables you to track time in seconds.

When you are ready to begin, start the timer.
- Start counting out loud as fast as you can and record the amount of time it took for you to count to 26.
- Reset the timer and say the alphabet out loud. Again, record the time it took to execute this simple task.

The total time for both tasks should be between ten and fifteen seconds.

Now let's try to disprove the long-standing myth about being more effective by multitasking.
- Reset the timer
- Count to 26 and A to Z in multitasking mode, i.e. 1A, 2B, 3C and so on.

Most people quit before making it to 8H and by then, the time has already exceeded the total they previously recorded by doing the tasks separately. Keep in mind that this task is very simple, so just imagine when the task is complex and we have to go back and reread multiple pages or even documents to get back on track.

The reason multitasking is less efficient than most people believe is because we cannot efficiently process more than one data-set at once. Furthermore, our cognitive processor can only deal with a limited numbers of variables at once. Our brains are powerful, but there are certain limitations we have to live with.

Below is a quote by Dr. Greg Wells on the physical effects of multitasking.

> *"STOP MULTITASKING, START SINGLETASKING*
>
> *If we try to multitask, we end up shifting the blood flow between locations and never giving the brain what it needs to get a single job done properly. Make it a daily routine to carve out an hour each day to focus completely on your most important task until it is either complete or you are out of time. Then move on to the next task."*
>
> *"**A study by Dr. Glenn Wilson from the University of London** showed that people who multitasked while performing cognitive tasks experienced a temporary drop in their IQ, similar to having missed a night's sleep. Bombarding our brains with information slows them down."*

As we continue to evolve AI and make computers faster, they will surpass the computing power of our brains, but they will only be able to emulate emotions, not feel. Having said the above, there are, and will be more and more, similarities between our brains and computers.

One thing to remember is that computers are now able to reprogram themselves. We also, as humans, are able to reprogram ourselves. It is not always obvious, but reprogramming our subconscious minds will alter our initial reactions, thus affecting our present and future realities.

We will see how to reprogram ourselves as well as how to benefit from it in the next chapter (The Power of Words).

> SUMMARY
> We have looked at brains and their astonishing similarity with computers and discussed how the more powerful they become, the more the resemblance is shocking. As artificial intelligence develops, we will see more and more computers execute complex tasks better than humans as humans can only process one set of data at a time. Reprogramming the subconscious mind is a key concept going forward. Let's not forget our unique abilities: We are able to love and be happy.

"Handle them carefully, for words have
more power than atom bombs."

Pearl Strachan Hurd

The Power of Words

MOST PEOPLE WHO KNOW ME would tell you that I've been born with the gift of the gab. In other words, I am extroverted, very much so, which in itself is a great quality to have in this day and age. But there is a flip side to this great quality, and uncontrolled, it can lead to many unfortunate situations.

Two years after I finished the curriculum for my master's degree, the head of the program hosted an alumni reunion at his home. John was a great person and I liked him very much. John was also known to push his students to the limit, and admittedly, it did make us better. During the event, in an effort to push me to finish my thesis, he threw what I felt to be a spear directly at my heart. The comment was: "Al, why aren't you finished yet? You are dragging your feet! Look at Chantale [an MSc student]. She finished her thesis in eleven months."

Without thinking, I retorted and made a comment which John's wife overheard that I regret to this day. Within six months, John and his wife were divorced, and I have paid dearly for this uncontrolled comment. I lost John's support from that day on, and it took me much longer to finish my thesis, not to mention a lot more work. To this day, when I think about what happened that day, I feel bad.

Not only do words matter, they are always influencing your subconscious, your attitude and ultimately your life's outcome.

One of the greatest discoveries of our modern era is not that we have gained the ability to conquer the moon or even that we made it to Mars; it is the realization that the subconscious has far more power than we ever thought.

We know beyond any reasonable doubt that the subconscious is always operating in the background, and most importantly, it can make us sick as well as heal us. The subconscious mind runs everything that we take for granted. It can speed up our hearts if it perceives a potential threat that we have not yet seen, and much more. I do not claim to be an expert on psychology, but merely through some observations from a layman's point of view, this all makes sense.

The words we sometimes use in the way we think or talk to ourselves can greatly affect our subconscious minds. We need to choose our words wisely. One of the most observable traits of successful people is that they seem to have positive attitudes, no matter what. Therefore, if we want to be successful in whatever we undertake, we should keep positive attitudes at all times.

All of the above brings the concept of reprogramming ourselves and influencing others.

As our parents raise us, they try to instill in us the knowledge they acquired throughout the years. As young children we take it all in, and it is a great period of learning, where we supplement our programming and become more knowledgeable. During adolescence there is a phase where young adults go through changes in their bodies and their learning ability is somewhat suspended temporarily, but eventually we all go back into learning mode.

Getting back to the concept of programming, the thoughts we perpetuate and the words we use will affect our subconscious minds and in turn affect our programming. In other words, if someone has formed a habit of negative thinking, it will usually give a negative connotation to all encountered situations. In this case the brain is subconsciously in the habit of looking at reality in a negative way, and at the root of all its negative thinking there are negative subconscious beliefs.

The problem with subconscious patterns is that we take them for granted and believe them to be the truth of who we are. Our perception again becomes our reality. However, the truth is that "subconscious" patterns are simply thought patterns that have been emphasized so many times that they've become imprinted as an "auto mode" of functioning.

There are some beneficial negative patterns, such as the child getting his hand burned on the stove. This will create an everlasting imprint on his subconscious and instinctively the child will stay away from a hot stove. Other examples might be walking in front of a speeding car, or insulting a stranger for no reason—there are many similar negative patterns that are beneficial, but for the most part, negative patterns are not desirable. We can become free of negative subconscious patterns in our minds by becoming aware of them and disassociating with them through lack of interest and attention. In other words, we can reprogram the subconscious by consciously choosing different thoughts and words, which will override the existing patterns that were previously imprinted.

There certainly has been lot written on the subject of which comes first; the thoughts affecting the subconscious or the subconscious affecting our choice of words.

I am sure that there are people who will have a better perspective than I have, but for the better part of my life, I can attest that on my entering into any situation, the outcome has been greatly influenced by my state of mind.

Without pushing the blame on our parents and school teachers and relatives, I believe that they had a lot to do with the initial input in our subconscious minds.

Many of the patterns we learned from childhood through observation and repetition have formed thought patterns on our subconscious minds and in our quest for happiness and needing a starting point we will act based on these established patterns.

Spoken words create imprints on the subconscious. Our choice of words is in direct alignment with our attitude. A positive attitude will engender positive thoughts and words, which will determine our audience's perception of who we are.

The subconscious plays a large role in happiness, as it influences our thoughts. We already agreed that for most people, perception is reality, therefore a sequence of events takes place depending on our subconscious patterns. If you are positive in your thought patterns, you will have a positive attitude and will use positive words, which will, in most cases, engender positive interactions. The reverse is also true, where negativity will trigger negative interaction and in the same way our first example created a positive wave, it will create a negative wave. The glass half-full or half-empty is the best example.

> *"Stay away from negative people,
> they have a problem for every solution."*
>
> Albert Einstein

All of our lives, we continue to learn and accumulate knowledge, which greatly determines how we will react to any given situation. Obviously, the response to a situation will affect the present moment as well as the future. This is best illustrated by a simple situation that happens to most of us from time to time.

At a coffee shop, while waiting in line, and depending on one's upbringing and subconscious patterns, one might turn to the person next in line and start a conversation, eventually getting a smile, a business card or even an invitation to sit together and develop a much deeper understanding of the other person's background. In the same situation, another person may stand in line and say nothing, and later sit alone and get on with their life without further interaction. In the first case, the individual may have altered his future by merely having interacted and found that the person he met is the HR manager of a firm that is presently looking for the type of talent he or she possesses.

Words put into a specific sequence form phrases that can be made into affirmations. Many books have been written about positive affirmations and God knows how powerful affirmations are. When repeated on a regular basis, these affirmations create thought patterns on our subconscious, which can change attitude and much more. This book will not dwell on affirmations, but merely suggest their power over happiness.

As mentioned earlier, there are three kinds of energy a human controls: Thoughts, Words and Actions. All three are usually in a logical sequence that determine the ultimate outcome of our lives.

The thoughts we harbor affect the words we choose and create a directional and proportionate reaction from the receivers. In other words, our choice of words describing a situation will be interpreted by our audience and will trigger a response, positive or negative according to our choice of words. This influences the audience's frame of reference about our character.

Most people would rather keep company with positive people simply because positive people make others feel better about themselves. It is in most part subconscious, but the feeling is real. If we pay attention to our entourage, we notice who are the people-magnets, and if we take the time to observe their behavior closely, we will identify the trait. A positive attitude is usually a subconscious method of acting and reacting, although it can be nurtured and controlled. With repetition, our thought patterns will change, as will our attitudes.

When we think in a certain way, the reaction to an event will directly and proportionally go in the same direction as our subconscious thought patterns. For example, we cannot easily anger someone who only thinks positively. Sure, if we threaten or insult him or his loved ones, we may get a negative reaction, but under normal circumstances we will be hard pressed to get any measure of anger out of a positive person.

Words are powerful as they will greatly influence our life's opportunities and outcome. Together, thoughts, words, and actions will ultimately determine our life's path.

There are rules that are easy to understand, while some others are more subtle, but one thing I have learned is that we will reap what we have sown.

> *"By thy words thou shalt be justified and*
> *by thy words thou shalt be condemned."*
>
> Matthew 12:37

The power is undeniable and is seen even more in the influence of speakers, politicians, and lawyers. Words can influence the perception of most situations if used in a skillful way.

Have you ever tried to convince someone to do a task they were not prepared to undertake? Your choice of words can sway either way, depending on how skillful you are.

The greatest lawyers are the best example of word manipulation; used with finesse, their words can influence a jury to get the guiltiest acquitted.

The words we use will influence our subconscious minds and ultimately our present and future. Underestimating their power can be a big mistake, so by all means, use them wisely.

> SUMMARY
>
> Words are more powerful than an atom bomb. Not only can they hurt an adversary, they can wound loved ones even more. They can be used to reprogram ourselves and the people around us. Used in the proper way and on a consistent basis, words can attract into our lives the most unbelievable people and opportunities. Choose them wisely as they can build us or break us.

"The **Law of Attraction** is one of the
most powerful laws in the universe. What you
think about is what you bring about into your life."

Jack Canfield

It's Magical

I HAVE ALWAYS BEEN A fan of magic. In fact, magic has been part of my life for at least twenty-five years. As I travel extensively and have spent time waiting in airports and many evenings alone, it gives me lots of time to practice magic. My preference is what is called "Close Up Magic," and I use money as my preferred medium.

I have made many friends over the years – magic attracts adults as well as children, as we are naturally drawn to it.

Everyone knows that magic is sleight of hand, a trick, or a gimmick, but nonetheless, it will attract anyone nearby due to the mystery.

Here, I would like to bring your attention to another type of magic; the magic of life itself, and the magic we encounter over the course of our lifetimes.

There is something magical about life. Some people somewhat understand this while others go with the flow. The rare few take the time to understand it deeply. Most of us are influenced by the many people who cross our paths or by the authors whose books we have taken the time to read. I have been deeply influenced by two authors, who have given the gifts of their knowledge and wisdom to the world. Dale Carnegie was a pioneer who wrote one of the classics in the field of personal development, *How to Win Friends and Influence People*. His work is straightforward and practical. Anthony Robbins made a career from training people on how to influence their lives with positive thinking; first by believing, then by taking action. I have read most of Robbins' books and attended the "fire walk" seminar, which was truly life changing for me. Is it magical or is the magic just the consequence of what we believe? Robbins has changed thousands of lives, including mine. By changing what we believe, we can empower ourselves to make whatever we believe happen in our lives. This includes happiness.

Is it magical? It is certainly not sleight of hand or a gimmick. I hope to bring you into the realm of magic and real magic in this chapter—no tricks.

Dreams and aspirations will help us get through hard times as they are the fuel of our hearts and souls. Looking forward to the future to find refuge is a simple way to get us through low periods in our lives and in the grand scheme of things, it is not a leg of the trip that counts as much as the total voyage of life. We have all experienced great euphoria and likely have also felt down. Certainly some of us have been depressed at some point in our lives. Life is not always predictable and sometimes it will throw curves at us. It is then that applying the rules and giving it our best will make us stand out. It is then that believing we can do magic may help us endure the toughest times in our lives.

> "Logic only gives man what he needs ...
> Magic gives him what he wants."
>
> Tom Robbins

> "Those who don't believe in magic will never find it."
>
> Roald Dahl

It's all good to be satisfied with what we have, but there is nothing wrong with wanting to program what we would like to happen in our lives. We all have dreams and aspirations. Depending on our personalities, the way we deal with those aspirations and dreams will determine the level of happiness that we will achieve.

In this chapter I will take you through two concepts (believing and affirming) that form the basis of attracting whatever you desire in your life. At first it will seem magical or even mystical, but I hope by the end of this chapter you will have gotten a glimpse of what helped me get through my life. I have been grateful every day for having understood and applied these principles.

I've admired Einstein all my life, not because he elaborated the most important theory of our time (relativity), but because he was the greatest example of when we believe in something hard enough, we can make it happen. Einstein and his wife developed and mathematically demonstrated the theory of relativity. Many years passed before we were able to prove the essence of their theory in a particle accelerator in Switzerland.

There is a relativity to life. You may or may not believe it, but it is as real as gravity. We can bend life's outcome to our liking, a bit like Einstein's theory of relativity or at least part of it. In 1904 it seemed impossible when first explained, but many years after Einstein had demonstrated mathematically that a light beam could be curved, Orest Khvolson (1924) observed the phenomenon and in subsequent years, many others followed. How does someone go from thinking about something to making it happen? It's mind-boggling, but I will try to shed some light on this concept. Believing is the first step in making anything happen.

You can distort your reality by having a positive attitude and using your energy in the search of happiness. The more you believe it, the more resolute you are, and the faster you will curve your reality in the desired direction. Happiness will come to those who seek it. Without planning for happiness, it will only show up at random.

Most people believe that happiness is an outside force influencing us. In reality, this is far from the truth. Happiness is a state that is developed from the inside out. There are many influencing factors and we shall explore those in depth, but let's first look at the situations and opportunities that come to us and how we can influence the outcomes. We will focus mainly on happiness, though these concepts apply to many facets of our lives and how we can attract happiness for ourselves and those around us.

There are many forces that affect our lives and without voluntary scrutiny, they can be easily overlooked. Nonetheless, the magic of attracting what we want in life is available to anyone who takes the time to learn how it works.

One of the best books ever written on the power of belief is by Dr. Wayne W. Dyer, *You'll See It When You Believe It*. Dyer explained this concept very clearly. Simply put, when someone believes in something deeply, he subconsciously looks to prove what he believes in and by those subconscious actions, he will attract it to his life. On the flip side, when someone does not want to see or understand a situation for what it is, the individual will try to disprove whatever he is focusing on; his actions will also be in that direction and his disbelief will prevail. Clearly, a person who doesn't believe in happiness will have a tendency not to see the situation for what it is or will distort the situation to fit his belief. Dyers' book is a great read for those who want to explore the magic of believing.

I ask you now to take a leap of faith, at least a small one, until I finish the demonstration that magic (the laws of attraction) is real.

There was a man named Matt who worked for me several years ago. He had been in the Marines and was tall, strongly-built, and average-looking. Matt was married to a very beautiful woman, who, although also in her mid-forties, easily looked twenty years younger. When I initially met Matt and his wife, they looked like they were madly in love. But the recession forced his wife to leave her real estate job to seek alternate employment and the new job eventually pushed them apart. Matt was still in love, however, and after his wife left him, he fell into a deep depression. He was sure that he would never again find another woman who would make him happy. Eighteen months later, his job performance had declined to the point that it was no longer acceptable. His supervisor had tried everything he could think of to motivate Matt and get him out of the rut he had sunk into—all without success. In the end, his supervisor didn't know what else to do and most of Matt's coworkers felt bad for him. It was then that I decided to jump in and give it a last try to save Matt from himself.

Armed with my proverbial speaking ability and an exercise that has proven time and time again to work, I sat down by the water with Matt one afternoon and offered to help him find happiness again.

I have spent most of my life trying to share this exercise with whoever wanted to listen. Matt, amongst many others, is living proof that the laws of attraction work because the exercise worked for him as well. The laws of attraction are real and are as strong as gravity. The simple exercise Matt used is described in the following paragraphs, and if applied as prescribed, will make things happen in your life that you thought virtually impossible.

The template for this exercise is available at Fun2Work.com/book-support/, along with a detailed description and video.

- Take a piece of paper from a lined tablet or use a computer in Word or any other text editor
- On the top line write "What I want" on the left side
- On the right side write "What I don't want"
- Draw a line down the middle of the page
- In no particular order, write what you want to attract on the left side (we will later re-order by priority)
- Repeat the same exercise for what you don't want to attract in your life.

Once you have done the above, look for what I like to call the Electrician/Plumber Syndrome. It is rare to find a good electrician who is also good at plumbing; the same is true for a bodybuilder who is not somewhat narcissistic…or a 6'2" jockey or a 5' hockey player. Plainly put, I'm talking about mutually exclusive characteristics; tall and short; outspoken but shy. Look for opposite characteristics that may be mutually exclusive by nature.

Take the time to rearrange each column in order of priority, with the most important characteristic at the top. By looking at the most important attributes you would like to attract first, strong signals are imprinted in your subconscious. Having the list in order of what you want first reinforces this process. Do the same on both sides of the list.

Once you're finished, fold the paper in half along the middle line. For the next three to four months read the "What I Want" side four times a day; at breakfast, lunch, dinner, and before going to bed. DO NOT look at the flip side as the laws of attraction have no polarity, and you will attract what you focus on. Within three to four months, you will start experiencing whatever you have been focusing on. Some of you may have laid out your ultimate mate, the perfect friend, or your dream job. Whatever it was you were trying to attract, be attentive and you will see it start showing up.

Be careful what you wish for, however, as this is a powerful tool and it needs to be handled with caution. What I mean by this is that whatever you wish for will affect your life in the near and distant future. Looking for a soulmate when you are married may have dire consequences on your marriage, as can wishing for a car you cannot afford. Life will bring you opportunities to achieve what you wish for. If your wish list is too out of reach, the opportunity to make it happen may not be desirable or even legal, so be very careful using this powerful tool.

Back to our example of Matt. Although he was skeptical, Matt followed the instructions to a "T." I later saw Matt at a show in Louisville, KY and it was obvious that he was back from his depression; smiling from ear to ear, he was radiating happiness. I asked what had changed since we had last met. He responded, "I did not believe that the system you had explained would work, but ever since I've known you, you have never steered me wrong, so I decided to go along with it. What did I have to lose? I did the exercise and it worked! I have met the most extraordinary, beautiful, and intelligent woman I could have ever hoped for—it is absolute magic!" A few years later, he invited me to his wedding.

Believing that we can change the outcome of our lives has been proven to work. Try it; it will work for you as it worked for me and millions of others who have applied the method.

> "To accomplish great things, we must not only act,
> but also dream; not only plan, but also believe."
>
> Anatole France

Believing in happiness is also magic. When we start by understanding and believing that we are the masters of our happiness, it will appear in our lives like magic.

There is a word of caution to be said about retaining whatever we have attracted, and it is as powerful as the laws of attraction. We can create the life we dare to dream of and many people will get what they wanted, but deep inside they do not believe themselves worthy of the achievement, whether it is a raise, a promotion or an award. When they feel they don't deserve whatever they achieved, soon after receiving such an accolade, they will put into motion a sequence of events that will sabotage the achievement and they will eventually lose what they had gained. We have to believe it to get it and also believe we are worthy of having it in order to retain it.

Sometimes after success is achieved, we forget what got us there in the first place and start acting in a different way. Behaviors such as arrogance after achieving an unattainable goal would be an example. Remember where you came from; where you were before you attracted whatever you brought into your life, because it is as easy to lose as it was easy to attract, if not easier.

> "Very little is needed to make a happy life;
> it is all within yourself, in your way of thinking."
>
> Marcus Aurelius

SUMMARY

The law of attraction is a force greater than gravity, but many do not take advantage of it. Learning to attract what we deserve into our lives is a critical key in our pursuit of happiness. Here in this chapter we explored this undeveloped force that can change anyone's life path.

"There is only one happiness in this life, to love and be loved."

George Sand

Love: The Ultimate Power

IT IS MY FIRM BELIEF that all humans crave being loved and it is impossible to talk about happiness without touching on what drives most living beings on this planet.

The most powerful force on earth is LOVE. Without it, nothing would grow, no species would procreate and most important of all, the human race would not exist.

There are many books written about love. I loved Rhonda Byrne when she wrote the book *The Power*. I believe that her book is truly a gift to humanity and to our realizing that love is so powerful it can literally move mountains.

Most experts agree that love changes in time and is mainly a chemical reaction in our brains and bodies. I always thought that love was the driving force behind everything. During my last year at Montreal University, it was love that propelled me, like a mad man, to chase the woman who is now my lovely wife of thirty-five years. That was, and is still is, pure chemistry.

I believe that the best way to touch on the power of love is to compare our energy levels between when we do a task that leaves us indifferent and another task that we love. To illustrate this clearly, let's look at when we love to run. We will await to get off work to run and will expand much more energy running than we spent during the whole day at work and for some strange reason, we will be more energized and feel better than when we got off work... unless perhaps you work for a Fun2Work certified company! For more on this, please visit www.Fun2Work.com.

Whenever we undertake something we love, it requires less energy and time seems to go by much faster. Some people have done deeds that surpass human strength and normal abilities. Take for instance Mother Theresa or Mahatma Gandhi. They are both examples of human beings doing the impossible with next to nothing. The energy required to achieve such deeds is virtually immeasurable and just look at what they have accomplished for the love of one's neighbor.

> *"Love is the only force capable of
> transforming an enemy into friend."*
>
> Martin Luther King Jr.

We all want to feel loved and it is part of our DNA to love and be loved. Wanted or not, where there is love you will find happiness and there is a simple explanation for that. When we love truly, we accept the other for who they are and don't try to change them, nor do we put expectations on them or on their behaviors. That in itself generates the grounds for happiness. The absence of expectations will lay the foundation for happiness to happen.

When love is present, there are many events that are automatically put in motion that create the right setting for happiness to happen. Although love does not guarantee happiness, it does help create the right environment for each of us to create our own happiness.

> *"Love is when the other person's happiness
> is more important than your own."*
>
> Jackson Brown Jr.

The old adage that states that "Love is blind," describes exactly that phenomena. When we are in love with someone, we only see the positive side of things. When we drop out of love, we subconsciously look at every little thing that bothers us and most likely forget all the positive behaviors that were all we focused on not too long ago.

One day, our neighbor, Roger, came to our door and requested that I have breakfast with him the next morning. He said that he had something very important he wanted to tell me and it had to be off site.

My wife, Barbara, and I had become good friends with our neighbors, Annette and Roger. They had become our reference couple. Both teachers at the local grade school, they had been married for over twenty-five years and seemed very happy together.

The next day, I met Roger at our favorite restaurant where we often had breakfast together. We began talking and the discussion quickly turned to the last time we'd gone cycling together, or more specifically, it focused on the red-haired young woman we had spoken with before setting out on our twenty-mile ride. She was indeed a beautiful woman. Tall, slim, and very athletic-looking with an angelic face, she did stand out.

"Remember?" Roger blurted out.

"Of course," I retorted. "She was by far the most beautiful woman there, in fact the most beautiful that has ever taken part in any of our previous rides."

"Well," he said, "I am leaving Annette and moving in with Monique next week. She is just fantastic."

I was stunned for a minute, then I regained my composure and threw back, "Roger, you are fifty-five and she is barely thirty-eight!" Roger was a good looking fifty-five-year-old in great shape, but Monique was completely out of his league. I suggested that there had to be something big; a fault that he had missed, but Roger quickly replied that she had no faults. It was then that I knew he was in big trouble; completely blinded by love. The whole episode lasted about six months. Roger fell out of love and began seeing Monique for what she was, still very beautiful, but somewhat erratic. She threw fits out of nowhere and happened to be so jealous that it became unbearable. Roger crawled back to Annette and she made him pay every day for his misstep.

Annette was hurt in the process and she also fell out of love, at least for a while. Unfortunately, the relationship we had with our neighbors never recovered before we moved. It had become pretty awkward to see Annette pick on Roger for every little task he didn't execute to her liking. That was real proof that love can have a huge effect on how we perceive any situation or person.

Barbara and I have always been open and deliberately direct with each other and fortunately we never stack frustrations; we get it out in the open as soon as an issue or situation arises, sometimes to our friends' dismay. As we age... together, we have gotten much better socially, but any frustrations are dealt with ASAP. We call it "clearing the air." It is a simple routine of stating the issue and discussing the pain it causes the other. Most of the time, the problem is resolved instantly.

Barbara has attention deficit disorder. After our first phase of love, what can be called the chemical phase, I was taken aback by her approach to life. You may or may not know, but people with ADD can be a handful and until I realized she had it, our life was tougher. Once you understand the signs and symptoms, you learn to appreciate the absence of filter and discover how to deal with sometimes awkward reactions or situations. Barbara and I are still in love after more than thirty-five years. It hasn't always been easy, but if you keep the fire going you will always find the positive side of being together. Love is stronger than fire, but it does require a bit of maintenance to keep it humming.

A few years ago I stumbled on an interesting concept of love which takes into account the other person's language of love, According to Gary Chapman, the five ways to express and experience love that Chapman calls "love languages" are receiving gifts, quality time, words of affirmation, acts of service (devotion) and physical touch. ... According to this theory, each person has one primary and one secondary love language. I have tried this in our family and was pleasantly surprised how it all changed our perception of our interpersonal communications. In a nutshell understanding what makes the other person tick, helps greatly our comprehension of what makes them feel happy. If you are interested in finding out more look up Gary Chapman: *The 5 Love Languages.*

Notice that as we age, a favorite artist whom we absolutely loved may not be as appealing a decade later. When we change, our preferences will change also, so it is only natural then that certain things we previously loved are now annoying.

What we love and how we love evolves over time and just acknowledging that fact helps us push through the years.

> "Where there is love there is life."
>
> Mahatma Gandhi

While we play the game, we may go through ups and downs and the love might not be present at all times, but happiness, on the other hand, is always there to be enjoyed. It is a matter of making sure that despite whatever changes we go through in our lives, we stay aware and adapt to the ever-changing environment we live in.

SUMMARY

There are so many words written about love that this book does not pretend to be an authority on the topic. Suffice to say that nothing would live without love, and a life without it would have limited happiness.

"If you accept the expectations of others, especially negative ones, then you never will change the outcome."

Michael Jordan

Objectives vs Expectations

THE GOOD, THE BAD AND THE UGLY

I have always loved the phrase "the good, the bad and the ugly," not only because it revives joyful memories of the film from Sergio Leone, but because it applies so well to the topic of objectives versus expectations.

I have always put an emphasis on communication, to the point that some of my employees would point out that I did repeat myself, and many times I would ask them to confirm what they had understood. It is a bad habit, but it has helped me better understand who I interact with.

The habit comes from the "Lesson of the Concubine" in the book *The Art of War* from Sun Tzu. It is the most probing example that depicts the difference between an objective and an expectation and its dire consequence. I have included this extract at the end of the book, *Exhibit A*, for your reading pleasure.

With the experience I have gained over my many years of managing people in business, I have realized how easily a misunderstanding can lead to disaster. Hence, in business, as well as at home, it is imperative to clarify the difference between *objectives* and *expectations*, two very confusing terms that are often misused, or should I say used in the wrong place and time.

With this in mind, when I hire someone, I try as much as I can to put the candidate into a position where they don't feel they have to over-promise to qualify for the job, which eliminates the risk of starting the relationship on the wrong foot.

There are so many books dedicated to communication that it's impossible to pick the best ones. It is one of the topics most written about in business literature and despite this, it is most likely the most misunderstood.

The Good:

Expectations can be a very powerful source of motivation, inspiration, and guidance. In the following pages I will demonstrate that clearly-set expectations can be very powerful and motivating. I will also suggest a framework for when and when not to impose expectations and attempt to help you understand the implications of such actions.

There are times in our lives that expectations enable us to function with far more efficiency than otherwise. For example, when we get married, one of the basic promises is that neither will cheat on the other. That is usually a firm expectation from both sides, as it should be. Loving our kids unconditionally is in most cases non-negotiable, as well as many other situations that are part of being married. These expectations are very beneficial, as they help us function better in our relationships. The absence of expectations would leave a huge chasm of doubt and our lives would be a lot more unpredictable—therefore insecurity would ensue.

There are also situations on the job where expectations enable us to function better. It is a clear expectation that we will get paid a certain amount for the work we do. This certainty enables us to make other commitments in turn, such as to our landlord or banker for our rent and/or mortgages. The absence of such certainty would result in massive insecurity in our lives and certainly create a lot of doubt for our bankers. On the flip side of that coin, our boss expects that we will come in on time every day, unless agreed otherwise. It would be difficult to fulfill any commitment towards customers, if anyone could show up on the job whenever they felt like it. These customers in turn expect to be served according to the company's service level.

There are many expectations that are part of the job and there is also a category of commitments that is present, but to certain extent is more flexible. These commitments are objectives.

Objectives fall into the category of targets, which are somewhat more flexible. Contrary to our previous example where coming in on time is a firm commitment that may get us fired if we fail to comply, missing a sales target may affect our bonus, but in the short term is a more flexible target. In some cases, especially when we work for a small company, the budgeting process is done on a more ad hoc basis, which usually leaves more leeway for the result. In a public company, the budget is usually the basis for the promises made to the shareholders, who usually show no pity if we miss the projected revenue and earnings, which are called "market expectations."

When someone is hired, in an attempt to get maximum dollars, the individual may promise the world. In other words, they might present themselves as super achievers. This may actually convert what could have been objectives into expectations. In this case, after you have been hired as a super achiever, your boss may have turned certain objectives into expectations. Then when you fail to attain budget or fulfill daily duties, your future at that company may not be as bright as you thought.

"Perception is reality."

Lee Atwater

When a perception has created an alternate reality, a person may find himself in a different world. You may believe that you have been assigned an objective, but since you have oversold your abilities, your boss may have imposed an expectation on you. Not realizing this situation may lead to disappointment. In other words, if the two persons involved are not aligned on the same reality, the result will most likely not be satisfactory for either party.

How many times at work have you heard that the problem is communication? Most of the time in couple's therapy the problem revolves around communication as well. Is it a surprise that when someone's perception differs from another's that problems arise? How does that happen? Is the key or turning point in any relationship, either at home or at work, when an objective becomes an expectation of which the other party is not aware? Many problems may arise in this situation.

The Bad:

When expectations are left uncontrolled, it can lead to massive disappointment. As much as expectations are powerful, they can also be devastating. It is critical to understand where and when to set expectations, as they can lead to negatives outcomes and attack one's self-esteem to the point of no return.

When setting expectations, one must ensure clarity, and it is important that both parties clearly understand. Abstraction of marital expectation and showing up on time at work are usually hard expectations, while any other expectations that are discussed must be communicated in a very clear and concise fashion if happiness is to be the outcome. It is important to note that the repetition or acceptance of any situation will eventually turn an objective into an expectation, unless the situation is properly managed.

When a coworker has been putting together a specific report on time every week for more than a year, we will come to expect it without realizing it. If for some reason the report doesn't show up on time, one reaction may be to inquire why it hasn't been produced—the other may be massive disappointment.

Just recently when a month's closing did not come through on a Friday, it generated a massive wave of disarray amongst the financial staff, who had learned to expect the month's closing sales report on the last day of the month. No need to say that this expectation is quite firm, especially in a large public company. The amount of money spent to ensure that the company network is up and running ninety-nine percent of the time, along with the resources dedicated to maintaining the computer system and produce the reports, creates that expectation.

In a public company, reporting is not an objective, it is a hard expectation. A smaller company, however, may have deadlines for financial statements and sales reporting, so the target date may be more flexible, thus for them, the reporting date would be an objective.

The Ugly:

The ugly is when expectations and objectives are confused to be one and the same. Unknowingly, parents and managers alike sometimes view objectives and expectations to be equivalent. We will explore the concept and attempt to avoid this trap as the outcome of this confusion will only be negative. Expectations, as I will demonstrate, are usually hard stops; objectives, on the other hand are, or can be, a sum of multiple goals leading to a result in time—it is more a journey than a train stop. The failure to clearly differentiate between the two can set in motion long-term, catastrophic harm to children and relationships alike.

When kept under control, expectations can be a source of satisfaction and great happiness. What we expect from ourselves and from others will ultimately determine how happy we feel. Unfortunately, when left uncontrolled, the expectations that we set for ourselves or put on others can be debilitating and self-destructive. We therefore need to be very careful when we choose to set expectations for ourselves and others. Objectives, on the other hand, are somewhat more flexible—they are what we aspire to. We set goals and objectives knowing that circumstances may affect the outcome. In other words, they are not cast in stone and will not generate as much disappointment if not met. Expectations are more fixed and aren't really flexible. In our minds they are what we are owed and if they are not met, will always generate a certain degree of disappointment.

We will get into the details of what generates happiness in the next chapter, but to clearly illustrate this concept, let's take a few examples that will put expectations and objectives in perspective.

Let's take an example of two secretaries who both love their jobs and both have worked hard on a big project. The first woman thinks that working hard is part of the job and benefits the whole team. She takes pride in this achievement and expects nothing in return. Her boss goes by and gives her a nod for a job well done. She feels joy immediately and will go home that day feeling happy. The second secretary worked equally hard, but in her mind, she expects a reward. Her boss stops by and compliments her at length for the wonderful job she has done and even tells her that without her hard work, the team could not have accomplished what they did, but offers no reward or public recognition. The second secretary feels very disappointed.

Although the two secretaries went through the same scenarios, the perceived outcome turned out totally different for each woman. What was so different that one was filled with joy and the other was filled with resentment? The only difference was the expectations each had beforehand and the perceived outcome of their respective reward. By no means am I saying that we shouldn't have expectations. There are some areas that demand expectations. For instance, when we deal with our bosses, or as a matter of fact, with everyone we deal with, everyone should be treated with respect. It is not negotiable, and neither should it be. This is something we should expect and not have to compromise on. Another example is harassment of any kind. In all my business years I have always expected from all that work with me to have a zero tolerance for harassment and to report any instances where they experience or witness any form of it.

Expectations are needed but they do need to be communicated clearly and understood by all involved.

In order to generate happiness around us, it is possible to help others manage their expectations towards us. The closer the relationship with others, the more influence we may have over them, so we can even help manage expectations they put on themselves. Believe me, I have done this for over thirty years; helping others manage their own expectations. Not only did it help them be happy, it has made my life a lot more enjoyable.

We need to manage the expectations others have towards us, to ensure that they feel good about our behavior towards them. Every opportunity we get, we should ensure that we are clear on the expectations vs objectives that are put upon us. Clarifying the situation will help both parties generate the desired outcome. Both parties may agree on an objective, such as "I will come over to help you paint your living room... if I am back from my business trip on Friday." This is clearly an objective and it is conditional to your being back on Friday. What may be an expectation linked to this objective is that the friend may expect a call on Friday to let him know that you will not make it, but it was clear not to expect your contribution if you were not back.

When you were a student, how many times were you disappointed after getting twelve commitments from friends to help you move on a specific date and only a few showed up? Usually by the third time you begin to realize that expecting all of them to show up is futile. You quickly see that only a few loyal friends show up. You also learn that some friends have come to expect that you will show up when they move, and they would be very disappointed if you didn't. As everyone eventually realizes, this is a two-way street, and everyone feels better when they know they can count on you to meet expectations. In a case where you are not sure you can make it, it is imperative that you manage that expectation.

For some people, happiness is appreciating getting a hug before leaving for work and another when coming back at night. For others, it is that warm handshake when we get to work, the kind words from the clerk at the coffee shop, or the neighbor who gives us a smile as we are leaving for work. We will call these folks, the

"APPRECIATIVES" – They appreciate when their objectives are met.

On the flip side of the APPRECIATIVES, there is a group of people who expect their lives to always go the way they want and when it doesn't turn out that way, they feel something is not right—in essence, they feel unhappy. These folks create for themselves and others around them a set of expectations and when these are not met, their reactions may vary, but the outcome is the same: disappointment. We will call this group the "DEMANDINGS" – Most objectives are expectations for these people.

There is a category of people who cannot function without setting high expectations on themselves and others; many times referred to as: Type A personality or DEMANDING. If you are part of that category, all is not lost. There is a light at the end of the tunnel. Being a former Type A myself and thinking it was the right way to achieve greatness, I was arrogant and sometimes obnoxious. Keeping in the foreground our ultimate objectives will help us get back on track to our destinations. Our quest for happiness need not be a struggle. Once I understood that well-managed and rewarded objectives can be as efficient as solid expectations, my life changed for the better. Understanding the fundamental difference between expectations and objectives will change your life's perspective, as it did mine.

There is a side note to be made here: Not all people want to give 110% on the job. Working hard is a choice and usually happens naturally when you have found a job you love and are good at. It is important to note here that when you work on a job you love, it requires far less energy than working on a job you hate.

If you are the boss—well, it is your responsibility to make sure you have the right people in the right place. Upon finding someone who is not enjoying their job, you should evaluate if it is worth helping him/her to find happiness or helping him/her find a new opportunity better suited to his/her talents and preferences.

SUMMARY

The clear comprehension of the difference between objectives and expectations is a critical element of the creation of happiness. Since both are often mistakenly taken to be the same, it is not a surprise that many ventures start off in total happiness and end up in full disappointment. If not managed properly, objectives can become expectations and most of the time, the result will be disappointment.

"Your work is going to fill a large part of your life, and the only way to be truly satisfied is to do what you believe is great work. And the only way to do great work is to love what you do. If you haven't found it yet, keep looking. Don't settle. As with all matters of the heart, you'll know when you find it."

Steve Jobs

Your Purpose

I AM NOT SURE THAT I can pinpoint why it took me so long to find my purpose. Perhaps it was that sales and negotiation came so easily to me. My brother became a university professor, and year after year he was at the top of the student appreciation surveys. I guess he had found his calling. He always seemed to have it easier than I ever did. I realized in my late thirties that what made me the happiest was when I was helping others and even better was when I helped people to find happiness. It is then that my life started to be much easier, and that is what I have built most of my wealth upon.

Finding a purpose or mission in life should be our prime goal. It is a critical part of becoming a great player in the game of life. Our lives change when we find it. The stars seem to align when we have found the purpose of our lives. We will try to expand on this concept in this chapter.

Everyone knows somebody who seems to breeze through life, having found their purpose. They smile more, laugh more, and work effortlessly. Their attitude seems unshakable; in other words they seem to be happier than most people on a regular basis.

There are common traits amongst people who have found their purpose in life or we may call it their "calling." They appear to be in control most of the time and their actions are driven by what appears to be a higher power. Is it confidence or a resolute determination that whatever they do, they are on the right path and they can do no wrong? The least we can say about these lucky people is that they seem to have it better than most. Many of us know a few individuals who are constantly in control.

If you don't know of anyone like this, think of your local volunteers. This type of happy person is often involved in a non-profit organization. Mother Teresa is probably the ultimate example, doing miracles with almost nothing. These unwavering individuals who dedicate their lives to the betterment of others' lives have found their calling; they exude happiness and spread it to everyone around them.

We need not emulate Mother Teresa to have found our purpose. There are hills to climb and mountains to conquer, yet we should first tackle our own small challenges. I have personally found that helping others energizes me beyond belief. Helping others discover happiness makes me so happy that although I have a pretty busy schedule, I always find the time to help someone who needs guidance in finding happiness. I also made time to write this book, by no means a small feat for a businessman who constantly travels.

I would never dare compare myself to Mother Teresa, whom I admired very much. Her passing was a great loss for humanity. Each of us has a mission to fulfill and when we find it, our lives get better, easier and we feel more accomplished. Although there are many books written on how to discover one's life's purpose, I decided to throw in my two cents to prevent the distraction from overly complicated concepts that clutter the issue. I have a very specific view on this subject and it is the intention of these writings to help you discover your purpose by exploring yourself and discovering whatever your own mission may be.

In the later years of my life I have made a conscious decision to help as many people as I can to understand how happiness spreads around people who take the time to understand where it comes from. My happiness has grown exponentially since I reoriented my destination toward helping others achieve happiness … thus this book and all the tools that help promote happiness. All tools, templates, and quick reference guides can be found at: fun2work.com/book-support/.

I myself appreciate concise explanations and remember a famous phrase from Einstein that I've always liked: "If you can't explain it simply, you don't understand it enough."

I recently stumbled on an Internet video which caught my attention. It was a ten-minute clip that claimed it would help us uncover our life's purpose in five minutes. There is a bit more to it than that short video, but in essence Adam Leipzig was definitely on the right path in his simple demonstration:

1. Know who you are

2. Know what you love doing

3. Know who you do it for

4. Know what those people want or need

5. Know how they will change or transform as a result

Let's try it out. Get a piece of paper or something to record your answers with or you can download the template for this exercise at: www.fun2work.com/book-support/.

Questions	My Answers
My name is	
What I would choose to do if I had no financial obligations	
Who I do this for	
What they need or want	
How will they change or transform	

1. Know that we are all individuals and that we are unique, in the sense that there is no one exactly like us. You can have an identical twin, but by no means will he be truly identical. With

this in mind, take a deep breath and state your name, then write it down.

2. Close your eyes and reflect on the present moment and think about what you would choose to do if you had no financial obligations. Take a few deep breaths, then say it out loud, and write it down.

3. Knowing who you do it for is a little bit trickier. It is sometimes hidden under a layer of subconscious matter that has not yet been uncovered. During this exercise you will continue taking deep breaths in a slow and relaxed matter. For no more than two minutes, close your eyes and picture yourself doing what you love most doing. As you are visualizing yourself, observe who you are with, or who you are thinking about. Try to retain this information without breaking concentration. Once you open your eyes, write it down.

4. Knowing what they need or want is also a tricky exercise and requires a bit of reflection. Most people show up in our lives because they have something to give or take; it's all about looking beneath the surface and highlighting the things you truly have in common. Again, take a minute to reflect and write it down.

5. Understanding how they will change or transform as a result is usually easier, but still requires introspection. The result of your interaction with anyone will inevitably be a change, no matter how small. As the level of implication grows, the greater the impact will be on the individual or group. If you have found your purpose, it will be of greater significance. Once you have it, write it down.

Most of the time our purpose tends to have something to do with serving others; we usually are at our best when we are in the selflessness zone. Just keep in mind that when we are on the right path, life usually gets easier and time seems to fly...we simply lose track of time.

Having done the five steps above, most people get a glimpse of their purpose in life. In case you haven't, don't worry, just go to a quiet place and redo the exercises above. For some, the exercise needs to be on the spur of the moment, for others more time is needed to let the purpose surface. Try it fast, try it slow, but don't give up. Your life purpose is yours and yours only; it will come to you, just be ready to capture the thought when it appears in your mind.

It is very important to do this exercise in the moment—refrain from dwelling on the past or getting too far into the future. What is important is that you connect to your inner self.

Meditation is a great way to get in touch with your inner self and reflect on your purpose.

There are many good books on meditation and depending on your state of mind, you may want to explore the following:

> *Mindfulness Meditation*—Glenn Harold
> *Mindful Living*—Thich Nhat Hanh
> *Practicing the Power of Now*—Eckhart Tolle

Meditation is a powerful tool to keep us focused on our game. Reflecting on our lives on a regular basis helps us remain pointed toward our ultimate destination. It reminds us that we are playing the game without losing focus on what matters most.

I love the way Eckart Tole refers to the Thinker in his book *The Power of Now*. In a nutshell, when he talks about the "Thinker," he is referring to our egos. The ego talks to us in a constant stream of words or thoughts. It is easy to mistake the ego for ourselves, WE ARE NOT OUR EGOS. We do not talk to ourselves; we feel our thoughts and situations. Sometimes we hear words and even see movies in our head. These words and images come from our conditioned minds, previously referred to as our subconscious minds.

It is critical that we free ourselves from our minds in the pursuit of our purpose, as we may have imprinted negative thoughts on our subconscious minds, which will prevent us from seeing our true purpose.

Echkart Tolle's *Power of Now* is a great read for anyone wanting to free themselves from the noise and the past imprints on their subconscious minds.

Understanding how your ego affects your everyday life is a critical step in finding your purpose. This helps you create the grounds for happiness long-term.

Have you ever had a job where time went by so fast that the day seemed like a few hours and the week felt more like a couple of days? If you are part of the minority that have experienced this, congratulations! On the other hand, if you are still searching for this type of job, *What Color is Your Parachute?* by Richard N. Bolles is a great book to help you make sense of your life's preference and ultimately your purpose.

There are multiple exercises in *What Color is Your Parachute?* that can help us discover our preferences and put us on the right path to find our purposes. We simply write down our preferences; i.e. what we most like doing. It is important when doing so that you remain neutral and that your present situation does not dictate what you prefer, it needs to come to you naturally. In order of preference, list ten things you like to do most. The second exercise is to list the type of person you aspire to be or want to emulate. List five persons and the reasons they are your reference. Notice the common thread between the people; usually this will also point towards one or two of your natural preferences.

Reflecting on the two previous exercises is the first step toward confirming your natural inclination, which should point you in the right direction to discover your purpose.

The basic thread is fairly simple: The closer we are to our calling, the easier our lives get. Our jobs are not only easier, synchronicities start to surface. In other words, people show up at the right time and right place. Things start to happen, whereas before we had to chase everyone to get things done. If we pay attention, we will see it show up in our lives time and time again as we get closer to our purposes.

Another way to confirm that we are on the right path is the feeling that everything comes more easily. If we were lucky enough to get a good teacher while in high school, we could tell which subjects we were most proficient at. Usually it is an early confirmation of individual strength or aptitude. The easier it felt, the closer we were to our personal talent.

We usually instinctively gravitate to what seems easiest for us; not only is it a natural tendency which should be encouraged, but when a student seems to have a particular strength, it should be fostered.

Too many parents try to push their children in the direction they feel is a good way to earn a living, not taking into account the natural aspirations or strength of the child. There is no greater mistake to be made with a child or young adult. Pushing someone in a direction contrary to their natural preference will at a certain point turn against the individual and generate lots of disappointment, or at the very least, the individual will not live his life to fulfillment.

> "The meaning of life is to find your gift.
> The purpose of life is to give it away."
>
> Pablo Picasso

I wish for you to find your purpose if you have not found it yet. As we go through life, being aligned on our purpose enables us to reach a greater degree of happiness.

SUMMARY

While playing the game, finding our purpose will help us elevate to a higher dimension of happiness. Not only does finding our purpose help us find happiness, it also ensures an easier passage through the game of life. We all have a purpose and it gravitates around what our strengths are. Usually when we get closer to our purpose, life gets easier, time flies, and we feel that we are in control of our lives… of our game.

*"Happiness is not something you postpone for the future;
it is something you design for the present."*

Jim Rohn

Happiness

IT WAS SEPTEMBER 17, 1994. I was sitting in front of the fireplace in the den of our new home, just reflecting on how fortunate I was going from eating peanut butter sandwiches most of the time during my years in college and university, to having just bought a 9000 sq. ft. home in a great neighborhood.

I flashed back to the time where I'd tried to borrow $10,000 from my uncle to house and feed myself during my last year of college and got turned down because he did not believe I would ever pay him back.

A burst of gratitude overcame me—for my parents and the great values they instilled in me, and for Phil Cousin, who gave me a chance to learn an industry that had given me so much.

My heart filled with happiness and gratitude, as I looked into the fireplace and watched the random pattern of the flames, thinking, *Could happiness be that random that only the lucky get it and get to keep some of it?*

That moment created the motivation to embark on a voyage to find the origin of happiness. Although I was happy most of the time, happiness still showed up at random; I didn't understand *how* and *why* it would happen.

It is the lack of understanding of the game that makes it so random. I initially started by looking closely at circumstances when happiness showed up, and I paid attention to the finest details of why I felt so happy. I also noticed that there were different degrees of the happiness I felt and that the happiness was not necessarily proportional to what I believed was causing it. When we are unaware that we are part of the game and especially that the game has rules that need to be learned, happiness becomes unpredictable.

It soon dawned on me that what seemed to be random events or circumstances revealed distinctive patterns. It also became clear that expectations were a key element of the process, but that sometimes it went the other way, and they created disappointment instead. Have you ever heard the expression "promise short, deliver long?" In essence, when someone promises short, meaning they are absolutely sure that they will come through, and then works hard to beat their promise, this will inevitably create joy/happiness.

To name one company that has understood and applied this concept, Amazon always gives a later delivery date at which they believe they can deliver, and then they beat the date. Worst-case scenario, they deliver on time. I just love Amazon!

It did take a while for me to put it all together, but in the end, once we focus on the process that creates happiness, it turns out to be surprisingly simple. I am amazed that we do not teach this in grade school, it is so simple.

In my personal, as well as my business life, I have evolved these findings for over twenty-five years now. It has changed my life and created happiness in my family and my friends, as well as in all my business encounters.

In essence, when we see life for what it is and realize that it is a game that needs to be navigated by learning the rules, we understand how the rules of happiness apply, and it becomes a crucial element in our quest to our ultimate goal…happiness.

In more than thirty-five years in business, I have come across thousands of people and personally interviewed hundreds. Since it is my firm belief that it is impossible to keep customers happy if our workforce isn't, I seek happiness-seeking people who knowingly or unknowingly have mastered the game to some degree.

In all these years, I have come across very few who understood where happiness comes from, and less than a handful who took full responsibility for their happiness.

For those who seem to want more and always more, I pass on a tale: "The Seven Pots of Gold," in hope that the reader reflects on what is often the source of their lack of happiness. See Exhibit B.

We all seek happiness, albeit unknowingly sometimes, and we all have a way of interpreting how we feel.

You may find that my interpretation does not fit your reality and want to derive your own meaning from these writings. Happiness is personal, but I did find patterns that lead me to believe there is only one source of it.

Before I lose any of you, I would like to add that there are many roads that lead to happiness, but the mechanism by which we feel happiness seems to be very similar in every situation I have encountered.

Joy and happiness are not generated by circumstances, but by the mere evaluation of the perceived versus the expected outcome.

I recently came across a formula that summarizes this statement:

$$Happiness = Reality - Expectations$$

Happiness has recently been defined by researchers from University College London as a mathematical equation. In the many years since I became fascinated with the happiness theory, this has been the closest to what I believe to be the functional definition of happiness.

Researchers from University College London developed the equation after observing a group of participants who participated in a study where they played a game involving monetary risks and rewards. They then used the equation to analyze data from more than 18,000 people around the globe, which had been collected through a smartphone app.

Although the study seems to be on the right track, like all scientific studies there's a lot of fluff around the simplest ideas. Happiness is a simple equation between our reality or our perception of it and what we believe we deserve from life; our expectations.

When Lee Atwater said, "Perception is reality," he was not far from the truth.

Up to now we have looked at many influencing factors that create the environment needed to generate happiness. We will now dig deeper into *how* it is generated.

Happiness is always generated the same way—our perception of reality vs. reality itself.

To demonstrate this, let me tell you about a very good friend; a great business man and a mentor. We have been on many adventures together along the years and always enjoyed our time together, from selling equipment, to travelling to car shows, or simply drinking together and sometimes a bit too much.

My relationship with Michel Caron has always been the most pleasant, since we seem to have a lot in common and we enjoy many of the same things. Everything seemed to be going so well; he had great kids and a woman he loved dearly. He was happy, and luck seemed to be going his way non-stop. What more could a man ask for?

One day after selling one of his companies, he was on a ten-day trip to Italy with three other couples. On the first day, they were all resting at the villa, and Michel got up for a bathroom break, though his friends thought he was retiring to his room. About three hours later, the dog belonging to the owner of the villa they were renting was barking. The owner came over asking if everything was alright since the dog never barked. He was suspicious something had happened. Everybody looked at each other, unknowing, and soon realized that Michel was missing, so they set out to find him. A few minutes later, to their great dismay, Michel was found, face down, immobile on the stone walkway leading to his room.

After many operations and a whole lot of praying, Michel ended up quadriplegic. He had only a minimal use of the fingers on his right hand and could minimally move his right forearm.

It did take him a while to get the mental going again, but anyone who knows him will tell you that he radiates happiness. Now, that being said, one may wonder how this is even possible.

On a Friday morning, I sat down with Michel and asked him straight out. His story of overcoming his physical restrictions and finding happiness, despite his situation, is truly beyond inspiring. His story had to be an important part of this book.

Well, from Michel directly, here it is.

After the incident, I was hospitalized for ten days and operated on, in Italy. Wanting to get back home and get expert advice on my situation, I insisted on coming back home as soon as I could. The return flight turned out to be the longest flight of my life. I was hung from the ceiling of the airplane in a hammock-style gurney, and then they rushed me to the Montreal Neurological Hospital. On the third day in Montreal, after undergoing many tests, the doctor and her assistant came into the room with a set of long needles and for twenty minutes, poked at me everywhere. She finally stopped and looked at me. I threw at her, "Good or bad news?" She retorted, "No good news." It was then that I knew I was in deep shit.

After feeling helpless for the best part of three months, I started looking around me and saw all the love and support I was getting from my immediate family, Mona, my better half, and especially Sylvie, my eldest son's wife, who assisted me every step of the way through my convalescence. I started to pull myself together and appreciate how lucky I was. Though my legs and arms didn't work, my head was fully functional. It could have been a lot worse! In the hospital I saw first-hand two clans develop as I was getting better; first, the positives who were looking forward to a new life, albeit with new restrictions. But also, a new way to look at life. The second clan was not pretty to look at, feeling sorry for themselves and going deeper into depression every day. I decided that the first clan had lots more to offer. I made a conscious choice to be happy.

It was then that I realized I had to reset my reality. Feeling the love from everyone and having the support from my sons and the woman I love helped me start on a new venture. Fourteen months after the incident, I was asked to give a speech at the Royal Military College of St-Jean (see Exhibit C). In a nutshell, I highlighted the difference I felt before and after the incident. For example, during my speech, I asked Mona to get up. I asked the audience if they thought I was so lucky to have at my side such a beautiful and caring woman. Do you know how many times that people told me I was lucky to have Mona by my side? At least a hundred in the past year. Before my accident, I spent seventeen years with Mona and no one ever told me how lucky I was to have her by my side. It's like I have nothing to offer anymore, that she is with me by pity. Maybe I have a little charm although I am in a wheelchair? Maybe I'm still interesting? This summer, I was at the nautical club and a beautiful woman leaned over me and told me I was good looking. You may tell me she had no taste, she may have been drunk, but maybe I do have some charm left. Between you and I, I may have a bit of charm, but I am **so** lucky to have Mona by my side!

Besides having Mona, I have a multitude of friends and family who stood by me, visited me, encouraged me and gave so much of themselves to make sure I didn't have time to feel sorry for myself or get depressed. Without these people, I may have fallen into total despair.

I always had a passion for cars. Every year, I attend the Daytona 500 and the Montreal Grand Prix. Cars and racing have been a lifelong passion, which still exists in me today and being able to actively pursue these passions contributes to my happiness.

I also have my birds. I am fortunate to live by the water and have multitudes of birds that come and visit me every day. I have decided to feed them, year-round, which gives me a lot of pleasure.

Looking at where you are and setting realistic expectations and fighting with all you have to exceed those expectations is the key to happiness. You must change your attitude to see the good in everything.

It is undeniable that Michel is a passionate individual; whether it be birds or cars, he always goes full-out, in whatever he undertakes. You quickly realize when you visit Michel that he does love cars. His front entrance is never used—all visitors are brought in through the garage and walk by the original FORD GT40, the 2006 GT, and the latest 2018 Ford GT. The original GT is as it was raced in 1967 harboring the number 1, and there's an original Cobra and much more. Michel loves cars so much that his office has a glass wall looking into the garage.

Underneath the house is a racing sanctuary, with racing memorabilia of F1 and NASCAR, and a special tribute to Gilles Villeneuve's racing career dating back to the years he was racing snowmobiles.

As previously stated, being happy comes from inside and is fully under our control. There are no better examples than the one above. Happiness can come from whatever ignites your passion, but it does require some effort.

Under tough circumstances, it is more obvious that the choice we make to be happy is not always an easy one. Our natural instinct is to always want more. Without controlling our natural urge of wanting more, especially when facing massive limitations, without resetting expectations, happiness is impossible.

It was our desire to be better that got us out of caves and gave us the drive to want to be constantly better off over the past millennia. This trait made us who we are today and ensures that most likely our descendants will have a better life than we had. There is a flip side to that trait, however, which left uncontrolled will generate frustration at best and chronic unhappiness at worst. Left uncontrolled, the quest for *more* will inevitably lead to unhappiness as there will always be someone with a bigger house, a bigger boat, a taller building, or a better job.

We can appreciate this trend with children who are given everything they ask for as they are growing up, without any sort of control. More often than not, it does not end well. As mentioned previously, a repeated situation will eventually become an expectation. When children always get everything they want, as soon as it stops showing up, disappointment will ensue. The reaction may vary, but only in the degree of disappointment.

There is nothing wrong in getting more, if that's what is driving us. What is dangerous is the misconception around the expectation of always getting more. Happiness is a journey towards our destination, which is maximizing happiness. As all journeys, preparation and the road we will use to generate happiness is critical.

As discussed in the previous chapters, there is nothing wrong with setting ambitious goals and challenging ourselves to achieve them. Problems arise when objectives turn into uncontrolled expectations.

Stefan Zweig, was quoted saying that "We are happy when people/things conform and unhappy when they don't."

I have found more often than not that people and events don't disappoint us, our models of reality do. It is our model of reality that determines our level of happiness or disappointment.

It is important to note that happiness is a journey, not a static state resulting from outside influence. Rather, happiness is the result of a sequence of decisions we make, which prepare the grounds for happiness to happen.

In a general sense, when we plan for happiness, we not only plan it for ourselves, but also for our immediate surroundings.

The urge to find happiness motivated my departure from Bartley as it has motivated most of my decisions since I was a child. This affirmation might not fit everyone's view on the subject, but having spent so many years searching for happiness, it is my firm opinion that there are not too many other models that better describe how we navigate our lives and our quest towards happiness.

I have helped numerous people throughout the years and often the people around me would wonder why I would take the time out of a very busy schedule to help someone that I don't work with or have very little relationship with. I have said it many times: I believe in Karma and it brings me joy to help people. I often get in trouble at the Home Depot for helping a stranger to choose a tool. Yes, I am a tool maniac. My wife would tell you that this a gross understatement. After she asked me to build her a small woodworking shop, the shop I ended up building her more closely resembles a small factory than a home shop. Tools bring me pleasure. I love doing things with my hands, it is the way I find relaxation in my life. Do I need the biggest tool chest Snap-On makes? Surely not, but I love tools, so I do have Snap-On's biggest tool chest and it brings me joy to buy the tools and even more joy to use them.

As Abraham Lincoln said, "Most folks are about as happy as they make up their minds to be."

Earlier in the chapter, we talked about expectations being the emotional interpretation of the formula that the London study has been describing. In other words, mentally we emotionally rate our target or expectation on a scale from 1 to 10 for a given set of circumstances that we feel we are owed (figure 1). On that same scale we evaluate what we are feeling or getting from that situation. When the expected result is met, a good feeling is perceived (figure 2). When it is exceeded, it will generate a proportional feeling of joy, the farther down the scale it is from the target expectation (figure 3). Also, being away from the target in the opposite direction, not meeting what we expected will also generate a feeling, but this time of disappointment (figure 4), also proportionate to the distance from our target expectation. Downloading these worksheets from Fun2Work.com/book-support/ or watching the video will help with comprehension of this concept.

Figure 1

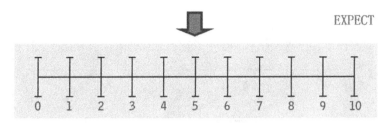

Figure 2

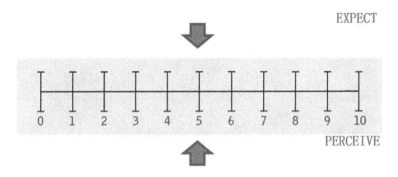

Figure 3

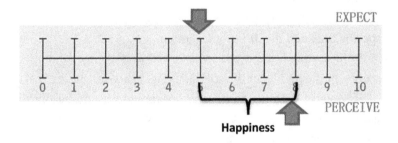

Figure 4

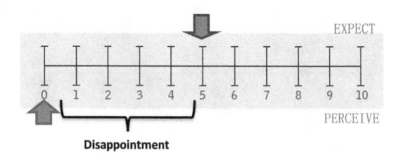

Figure 5

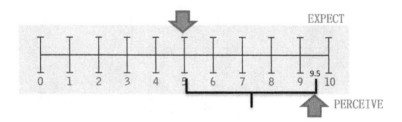

We may expect that our mate will put the garbage out on Sunday night since the garbage pickup truck will roll by at seven the next morning. If this has been done on a regular basis, we will have a tendency to expect that it will continue to be done at a specific time and that it is not forgotten.

In most cases if the expectation is well set, the targeted number will be in the middle of the scale, i.e. (Fig. 1) above.

If Monday morning comes and our spouse has not put out the garbage, when we see the truck go by, it will most likely generate a feeling of disappointment as illustrated in figure 4.

Expected 5 result 0, you will feel 5 units of disappointment.

There are several ways to illustrate how happiness is generated. My favorite is by using your spouse or kids if you have any. Keeping the scale previously described in mind, picture in your mind or write on a piece of paper the scale we have described in the previous paragraph or download at Fun2Work.com/book-support/. To make the example simple we will assume an amount for a gift given at Christmas. If your gift is of greater value, you should use that amount, but when asked what amount most people give to a twelve-year-old, on average over the past three years, it is usually around $150. The amount has no bearing on the amount of happiness generated, therefore your amount will be fine. Calculate on average how much you have given at Christmas in the past three years and keep that amount in mind; it will be our reference point for this example. This amount is our reference amount, so on our scale it will be positioned in the middle above the number 5 on our scale (Figure 1). Now comes the twist: This year you won the lottery and you feel very generous. You haven't told anyone in your family of this surprise income.

Because of your winnings this year, you decide to give a bigger gift. For your child, you may feel extremely generous and buy a very expensive drone along with a computer (drone simulator), spending well over $3000. For your spouse, you may decide to buy his or her dream car. In both cases, the expected amount is around 5, i.e. whatever amount they are expecting, when they receive their respective gifts, they will both evaluate their gift anywhere from 9 to 10 as per Figure 5. In other words, what is received versus what was expected will generate a proportionate feeling, on the positive side of the scale.

Now comes the critical step. Since the target (expected gift) has been surpassed by so much, the expected amount for the following year will increase dramatically. Therefore, it is essential to manage the expectation for next year, i.e. this was an extra-ordinary gift, please do not expect this another time, we are back to usual.

Another way to picture this and prove this theory is to wrap two dozen pairs of socks in a PlayStation box. When your child unwraps the gift, his excitement may reach 9, but upon opening the box and seeing socks will definitely turn into disappointment.

The take away from this example is this: Expectations adjust up or down with the evaluation of each situation encountered. Managing expectations is the only way to ensure happiness over any sustainable period of time.

I have found no other sources of happiness other than meeting or surpassing expectations. It is so simple that it seems unbelievable, but when you reflect on every time you felt very happy, you will find that your expectations were either met or exceeded. When you feel disappointed, look back and you will find that you were expecting something that did not materialize.

As I've grown older, I have come to the realization that we are instinctively seeking happiness, in all its forms. Not knowing what creates happiness is probably the most frustrating thing anyone can experience. Anyone who has had a baby would tell you that a crying baby can drive you crazy, not because of its cry, but because you don't know why it is crying. Feeling helpless when faced with a situation generates frustration; not understanding the situation subconsciously creates a void that will not feel right. The accumulation of frustration will modify our outlook on life, thus changing our behavior and in direct consequence, it will change our life outcomes.

Happiness is free, it only needs a bit of caring to spread around us and most of all it will come right back at us since it will primarily spread around the people we know. Nonetheless, suffice to say that when I spend time helping others figure out how happiness works, I am happier than I have ever been in my entire life.

"Success is not the key to happiness, happiness is the key to success. If you love what you are doing, you will be successful."

Albert Schweitzer

A few years ago, my son called me up and asked me to meet to discuss a job offer he had received. The job required him to move to the USA and he would make two times his present salary and in two years, most likely three times.

He tried to get me to decide if he should take the job. Here is how I answered:

"The job offered is in Merger and Acquisition, which is the job you had two years ago and you quit because you were working 90 to 110 hours a week and had no life. Having said that, when you get up tomorrow morning and all you think about is the excitement of working again in M&A with an exciting team from whom you will learn and become even better than you are today, well, give me the key to your apartment, jump on a plane and go to the US. I will take care of all that is necessary to send you your stuff.

"On the other hand, if you wake up tomorrow and all you can think about is the huge salary increase, you may want to take a deep breath and give a good hard look at what your future will look like."

It is not possible to play both sides of this decision, but my son chose not to move and to focus on living. His quest towards his ultimate goal got him back on track at the top of his game. As captains of our own lives, we do have the choice of path. Keeping in mind that the ultimate goal is to maximize happiness and making our decisions based on this, will help us arrive at our destinations. A few months later, my son met Stephanie, the love of his life, who's beautiful, smart, and above all, she has a heart of gold.

Had he pursued money, they would have never met.

The game will throw curves at us and sometimes tempt us into making choices that would steer us away from our fundamental values and/or our purpose. It is important to evaluate these opportunities with great care...

> "Money Can't Buy Me Love"
> The Beatles

SUMMARY

We explored a system explaining how we perceive happiness and how, when managed with care, it can generate more often than not the fertile grounds for happiness to be felt.

Happiness is our pursuit—there is no other quest that will soothe our minds. We all want to love and be loved, which is also a prerequisite for happiness.

When we have played the game well and achieved a great state of happiness, the next step up in the game is to appreciate what we have.

"Happiness cannot be traveled to, owned, earned, worn, or consumed. Happiness is the spiritual experience of living every minute with love, grace, and gratitude."

Denis Waitley

Gratitude

IN THIS CHAPTER, I HAVE drawn on many authors who have had profound thoughts on the subject of gratitude.

I will interject here and there with my thoughts to give it a personal touch, appreciating all the hard work and reflection of many great thinkers.

Gratitude has to be the greatest quality a man can possess. Even if we were to have everything we ever wanted, if we do not appreciate it, it will not weigh much in the balance of our lives. Part of the joy of having something is acknowledging where it came from and how it came to be. In most cases, this can be summarized by gratitude.

> *"Gratitude is not only the greatest of virtues,
> but the parent of all the others."*
>
> Marcus Tullius Cicero

The feeling of gratitude is the appreciation of how we achieved what we have or whatever we have accomplished, and who helped us along the way. Gratitude enables someone to be humble and in most cases, will be a determining factor on the longevity of whatever we possess or think we possess. In our lives we will achieve a status level and if we forget how we actually obtained such status, it can be taken away as fast as it was attained.

> *"Health is the greatest possession.
> Contentment is the greatest treasure.
> Confidence is the greatest friend.
> Non-being is the greatest joy."*
>
> Lao Tzu

> "Gratitude is what we radiate when we experience grace,
> and the soul was made to run on grace
> the way a 747 runs on rocket fuel."
>
> John Ortberg

> "Give yourself a gift of five minutes of contemplation in awe of everything you see around you. Go outside and turn your attention to the many miracles around you. This five-minute-a-day regimen of appreciation and gratitude will help you to focus your life in awe."
>
> Wayne Dyer

Today, I live on a two-acre property on the water, in a suburb facing Montreal. The wildlife is just amazing and every day I wake up as the blinds gradually rise and expose the animals wandering around our backyard ... every day.

When I wake up at home, my heart is filled with gratitude as I pause and look at the St-Lawrence River, the wildlife, and the nature.

> "Gratitude is the healthiest of all human emotions. The more you express gratitude for what you have, the more likely you will have even more to express gratitude for."
>
> Zig Ziglar

I'm grateful for my health, glad I'm making people laugh, glad my wife still loves me after all these years, grateful my daughter has grown into the woman she is today, an accomplished recruiter at a well-known firm and someone who excels at photography—I still don't know how she does it, what a woman! I'm so proud of my son for having grown to be an astute private equity investor and know he will surely attain heights that I have not. I'm glad

I don't take myself too seriously and I'm grateful to be coming home every night.

Yesterday a friend called me to give me the bad news that his friend, a very successful consultant whom I had the privilege to have met two months ago in a quest to learn more about consulting, just passed away from a massive heart attack in the middle of the night. I am grateful every morning that I wake up and witness the wonders of Creation.

For the longest time, I have said that I am and have been the luckiest man alive, and I truly believe it. God has never given me the urge to get more than I could afford and never tempted me into anything I could not control and for that, I am very grateful.

Finally, I appreciate all of you who have decided to embark on this quest for happiness and have purchased this book, which is the result of my life's work and is also the foundation for the company that I have started to spread happiness to as many people as I can: www.Fun2Work.com.

> SUMMARY
> As we are able to live our life in gratitude, a whole new dimension of life opens up and opportunities for happiness multiply.
> Every day I am grateful for the life I have and also for everyone that is part of my personal and business life.

"Happiness is as simple as 1 2 3, it just needs a little caring in our thoughts, words, and actions to make it happen."
"In the end, it's not the years in your life that count. It's the life in your years."

Abraham Lincoln

Conclusion

I PERSONALLY AGREE WITH ABRAHAM Lincoln when he said that "Folks are usually about as happy as they make their minds up to be"... with a little twist of understanding and preparation.

Being the captain of your life, you are able to choose your destination and use whatever tools that are available to navigate your life ... the game.

At the beginning of this book, I made a promise to help you understand where happiness comes from and it is my intention to take all the tools and exercises I have explained, and bring them together to form a whole.

The pursuit of happiness for all of us is a voyage, an adventure that needs not to happen at once, but rather can be planned and nurtured. There are steps to be taken that I believe enable and enhance our chance of playing the game and achieving a happy life.

We are also responsible to better plan for ourselves and the people in our immediate surroundings to create a solid ground for happiness to happen.

In my life, I have always believed in Karma, and so my actions and decisions have been taken and made accordingly. I also believe that most individuals work with the basic decision pattern explained in these writings; i.e. seek joy/avoid pain. It has been always my first premise to believe that most people seek joy and that most have a good heart. Until proven otherwise, it has always helped me to trust and verify rather than assume otherwise. Taking life too seriously also has taught me that I was the one missing out, not the others. Life is a game and learning and teaching the game to our kids early will help them immensely.

I have covered lots of ground and it is my opinion that most situations in our lives are a whole lot simpler than we make them out to be. Without wanting to over-simplify what we go through in life, I guarantee if you apply what we have covered, your life will feel a whole lot simpler.

How we think and feed our subconscious minds will affect our life outcomes much more than might be expected. Keeping a positive attitude helps reprogram our initial reaction to any situation with which we are faced. The key word here is initial. Some folks would lead us to believe that we must be absolutely positive even though the boat we are on is sinking. If the boat is sinking, we must find a way out. I am a positive believer, but we must take action, if action is required.

Be very careful of what you attract, sometimes a very desired outcome comes also with undesired side effects. As cause and effect is in full force 24/7, what we wish for will inevitably come with some side effects. Some will be good, but some may not be as desirable.

The thoughts we harbor and the words we use will shape our actions and ultimately will influence our life outcomes. Keeping a positive attitude will help us control our lives. It also sets the stage for happiness for us and for the people who are part of our lives.

Using the laws of attraction to bring into our lives what we desire will serve us well if we navigate life with humility and gratitude. Never forget where you came from and how you got what you have.

One of the most important foundations of happiness is understanding the significance of expectations and their usage. Never confuse objectives for expectations. In a family setting, uncontrolled expectations can be devastating for the recipient. Even before I realized this, I was fortunate enough to instinctively never put expectations on my children and they have both graduated from university and have successful careers. At a very young age, when they both had no clue what university was, I started planting the seeds. Many times a year I would ask them what university they would go to. I talked about how their mother and I met on campus and many times, we would visit Montreal universities and colleges. As time went on and they became aware of what university was, they became more conscious and when the time came, it was not a matter of going or not, it was a matter of which university to go to. The more we think about anything, we will attract it. Using the tools described in this book just accelerates it.

Finding our purpose is also a cornerstone not to overlook. Being in the wrong place, wrong job makes it more difficult to find happiness. Happiness is controllable to some extent, but we need to help the stars align with our purpose, which in itself gives meaning to our lives. Having found our purpose simply increases the degree at which we may feel the happiness from any situation on our way to our ultimate destination.

Finally, for those who have skimmed through the book, here it is:

Happiness is the result of understanding the game, and managing what we expect out of life in detail, as well as what we expect from ourselves and the people in our immediate surroundings. Managing expectations and also analyzing what we are experiencing with a realistic view will in most cases generate the required grounds for happiness to happen. Happiness comes from the inside out, and we have never felt happiness or joy if what we expect does not happen as we had expected or come within a close range. See Figure 3 on page 119.

The last word would be to highlight that gratitude in all its forms is the ultimate source of happiness.

My hope is that this book will have helped one person to get closer to happiness. My wish to you is that you live a life of happiness and gratitude

From the bottom of my heart, thank you for having taken the time to explore happiness through these words.

Live well and be happy.

Always have an attitude of gratitude.

Write to me at: al@Fun2Work.com

Thank you, *Al*

Acknowledgement

Most people can pinpoint those who have influenced their lives, especially at turning points. For most, it will be their parents, for others school teachers. My life has been influenced by a few people who have given me direction and provoked a fundamental shift in my life.

First is my mother, who passed in 2006. She instilled in me the values that made me who I am today. My wife Barbara, who has taken care of our family and relentlessly raised our two beautiful and fabulous children. My son and daughter for being so great, for whom it has been a pleasure in taking credit for having raised such wonderful children.

In my business life my first partner, Phil Cousin gave me the opportunity that very few people ever get and for that I will always be grateful. Thanks to him I have learned an industry that has benefited both our families.

During the last thirty-six years I have been blessed to have had the most amazing assistants anyone could ever ask for. First, Mme McDonald who had a "joie de vivre," which kept everyone happy around her. Last, but certainly not least, Mme Prince. Laurie has been the most amazing woman I have ever met in my business life. She has made everyone that got to know her a better person, including me. My life has been so much better and for that, I will be forever grateful.

As I was writing this book, Laurie, while battling cancer, helped me every step of the way to finish the writing and editing. Without her support, this book would not have been published. Her help and support putting together Fun2work.com to make happiness available to as many people as possible has been our common quest for a few years.

Last, and again not least, you who have purchased this book and dare embark on the voyage of creating happiness.

From the bottom of my heart:

THANK YOU,

Al Dorais

A Brief History

I was born in Quebec, Canada, in a small town in the Eastern Townships, into a middle-class family. My father came from a family of electricians, his father and all four of his brothers worked in the family business. My father originally worked at the family business, but it didn't take long before the entrepreneur in him propelled him to start his own business. With a $500 loan from his father and a warrant from the man who raised my mother, my parents started a furniture store across the street from the family business. The logic behind that was that whoever was building a house would also need an electrician and eventually would also need furniture to put in the house they had just built.

Everyone needs a break in life, and in my parent's case, the opportunity came from my godfather. He was a wise man who had raised my mother after my grandfather had remarried. He was retired but had spent his life selling furniture in a city sixty miles from where we lived. He had contacts with the major suppliers with whom he had a long history of business; he thoroughly knew the business and was a well-respected business man, which meant a lot back then.

My parents built a small furniture store and to minimize cost, we lived in the back in a modest apartment. I only remember it from seeing photos as I was too young back then to have any real memories of my own. In fact, I was born in the back of that furniture store. My father and mother later bought a house close to a school about three miles away from the store and eventually, they built a huge store in the same town.

During the summers, I would much rather spend time with my dad than go play with other kids. My father went to the office on Sundays before hitting the road early the next morning and often asked me if I'd like to come along. With the greatest of pleasure, I always eagerly accepted his offer. I typically wandered around the huge store, which spread along the whole block and at the time appeared to me like a landing strip.

Once I'd had my fill of jumping on beds and sliding down carpet strips for a few hours, I reconvened with my father in his office. His briefcase would be on the right corner of his desk and as I came in, he would put down the book he had been reading. Looking back now, it actually seemed like he had been waiting for me to stop playing so he could share what he was doing with me. I started traveling with my dad when I was just ten years old, and I have to say that generated memories that have stuck with me all through the years.

Back in 1971 when I was twelve years old was when I first noticed that my father was reading Human Resource books, though this was way before HR became mainstream. I did not clearly understand what he was reading, nor did I know why he was reading about HR, but one thing I vividly remember is that most of his employees loved my dad. This was further acknowledged when he passed three years later, and most of his employees showed up at the funeral. Many of these employees were not making enormous amounts of money and had still taken the time and effort (and expense) to send flowers. Despite my young age, I wondered why he was appreciated so much by his employees. I now realize that he simply created happiness around him, everywhere he went.

As I grew up, I heard many stories about my father—it's like that in a small town. Not only was it fun to work with my dad, it also became obvious as I grew up that he was well respected and appreciated all around town.

My mother was an extraordinary woman. She took care of our education and education we got... as much as we could stand. Today I am so grateful for all she taught us and for having enforced our manners. She got our elbows off the table, got us to use proper language and got all of us to sit up straight at the table. My father had the easy job of raising us, while my mother would tell us how we should behave. Our father only had to give us the *LOOK*, and we all knew very well what that look meant. My father applied only positive reinforcement and taught us that all actions had an equal and opposite reaction. If we didn't understand the rules, he would not understand our demands when it came time to ask him for a favor. I guess that's how life works... most of the time.

In the span of twenty-two years, my father built a very impressive business. He had three furniture and flooring stores, and in later years he also bought a golf course, which he used to tell my mother was his retirement fund. My mother was the accountant for our companies and did a great job keeping him fully updated on all financial aspects, including collections. When my father passed at the age of forty-two, my mother ended up CEO overnight. Unfortunately, it did not turn out well. I had heard my mother tell my father many times over that if she were to run the business, we would make a lot more money, to which my father would respond, "Yolande, thank you for counting our money, but the day you will have to bring in the money, you will change your tune," and her tune did change. Although it is not fair to make any judgments on how it turned out, the result might have been quite different had she not been afflicted with deep depression after my father's passing.

I was only fifteen years old when my father passed and for most part I was unaware of my mother's deteriorating situation. I was also struggling myself with my father's passing and not doing very well. Having spent most of my summers traveling on the road with him, I had come to be very close and attached to the businessman he was. When he passed, I have to admit that up to the time he was put into the ground, I was sure that he would rise out his coffin, at least I hoped so. I stubbornly insisted on staying at the burial site until they lowered the coffin and buried it. That is not recommended.

Losing my father left me in a state of shock. Before my dad's passing I had never worn a pair of jeans in my life, I'd always had a clean haircut, and a polo shirt was as close as I got to a T-shirt. However, from that point on and for the following four years, I didn't get a haircut and jeans and t-shirts became my preferred choice of clothing, much to the dismay of my whole family including my grandmother. I also convinced my mother that a one-year sabbatical from school was in order since I had gone through a lot in the past months. She surprisingly agreed, and I dropped out of school, planning to never go back despite the negotiation with my mother for just one year off. I thought I was so sharp back then, I could cut a tomato into thin slices. Because I was just fifteen, the school authorities didn't see it the way we did and told my mother that they would alert the police if I wasn't in school and they would come for me wherever I was and drag me to school until I was sixteen. My mother took me aside to explain the situation and to her great dismay, I ran away and only came back once I could legally drop out of school. My mother passed away at the age of seventy-one and on her deathbed told me she had never forgiven me for running away without telling her where I went. I had always hoped that it had slipped her mind and along the years, we never talked about it, but I knew I had lost my status of favorite son after that episode. She got to be much closer to my younger brother.

I was the eldest of the four children, and I believe my brother and two sisters were too young at the time to really appreciate or understand what our mother was going through. My mother went into a depression that took her to inexplicable depths and the business managers in place took advantage of her in so many ways. The businesses declined, some of them were sold for next to nothing, and within five short years, she had lost all that she and my father had struggled for twenty-two years to build.

During the early years after my father's passing, I became a first-class bum. I hung around with people who were not bothered that I didn't care about anything other than riding a motocross, drinking beer, and working the least number of hours possible to collect unemployment insurance. For the best part of those four years, I mainly slept straight through the mornings, rode my bike in the afternoons, played pool in the evenings and nights, and drank beer. Back then the Canadian unemployment rules were very pro-employee. I would work the minimum time necessary (roughly three months per year) and get laid-off to collect unemployment for eleven months. Once in a while, Ray, the owner of the fiberglass factory where I worked, would call for me to come in to do a special order. On rainy days I would go, which is probably why he would put up with my quitting every year around the beginning of summertime. I have to admit now, these were not my proudest moments.

During those carefree years, I always believed that my dad was somehow watching over me on a constant basis. There had been too many instances where trouble would pass right before or right after I had been there. One time I got into a race to a neighboring town and passed the local garage owner who had a Pontiac Grand Prix with the best tires money could buy. Upon my arrival he said, "I can't believe you passed me in that curve, I could barely keep my car on the road!" I had felt somewhat of a pressure on my car when I'd stupidly done that maneuver. Another time, I took a drunk hitchhiker for a ride on the hood of my Road Runner. Luckily the scoop held up and the passenger made it ten miles down a country road at over 100 miles per hour… I'm not proud, just lucky he didn't let go or the scoop didn't rip off my hood.

My life wasn't going anywhere, but I had found happiness in doing just about nothing useful with my life; I felt happy in my new reality. Once in a while someone would cross my path and a glimpse of the past would spring into my mind, and I would for a moment think of what it could have been if my father was alive. Then it would pass, and I got back to being happy with just about nothing.

One calm weekend, something happened which triggered a sequence of events that changed my life forever. We had driven thirty-five minutes to a neighboring town to visit my best friend, who was a doorman at a popular strip club in Granby. About an hour after I returned to my hometown, he was shot dead; a bullet to the chest and multiple bullets to the head. The next day we were alerted to the murder and learned that the police had no clue who had shot my friend. I set out alongside his whole family to find out who had done this awful deed. A few months later, another brother was found dead in his home, and finally, the bravest of the five brothers was shot and left in critical condition when coming out of a bar downtown—all of this within three months of the initial crime. It didn't take me long to realize that something was seriously wrong. I will admit, however, that it did take a long time for me to humble myself in front of my godfather. I finally went to him to ask what he would do in my place. He looked me straight in the eyes and said, "Son, since your father died, you have been lacking any sort of discipline, your life is going nowhere, and you look more like a bum than the young man you should be. You should enroll in the army!"

I was so scared I didn't really think too much about the solution he offered to solve my problem… staying alive was a priority. Within a few days I was in the recruiter's office in Sherbrooke, enrolling in the army just as he had suggested.

The funniest thing is that it almost didn't work out. The recruiter originally turned me down after I failed the psychology test. His exact words were, "You don't have the army profile." I don't know if it was fear-driven or out of fearless determination to get into the army to hide, but I quickly replied, "Sir if you don't let me into the army, within a year I will be dead or in prison. Please let me in."

The seriousness of my statement must have had a positive effect because instead of turning me away, he sent me on my way saying, "I will let you know my final decision within a few weeks." I was convinced that I wouldn't be accepted, after all I did look like a bum and I didn't have the eye of a tiger either. For sure he saw fear in my eyes and not bravery.

Two weeks later, good news came in the form of a train ticket, enrollment papers, and a letter indicating that I was accepted and requesting I show up the following month at the army base in Cornwallis, Nova Scotia for basic training.

Being accepted into the army gave me the greatest relief I had ever felt in my entire life. This would be a guaranteed refuge where no one could get to me. At the time I wasn't really thinking of the consequence of the life choice I had just made, I was simply happy my life was saved. I had no way of knowing at the time that it was going to be saved in so many ways, and ever since I came out of the army, I have told everyone that would listen that I have credited my life turnaround to my short stay in the Canadian Armed Forces.

Basic training has a way to refashion our body, mind, and soul... and so it did. Within six months I was ready to conquer the world and by that, I mean the army gave me a purpose and set me straight. I had cut my hair to my shoulders to look half decent before taking the train to Cornwallis, but within two weeks of enrolling, I was wishing that I'd gotten a crew cut beforehand. The army has a way of taking advantage of bums by not cutting their hair for a few weeks. Wanting to fit in and being refused a haircut just makes us want one even more desperately. This technique worked so well that ever since I got out of the army, when my hair goes over my ears just a bit I feel the urge to get a haircut.

So the army did save my life. I got out more quickly than expected with an honorable discharge. At enrollment I had omitted to tell the recruiter that my right knee was somewhat in bad shape due to an awful fall racing motocross. I was able to hide it because it didn't hurt unless I overused it. Basic training put a lot of strain on my knee and towards the end, my knee started swelling badly and hurting so much, I could barely walk. The sergeant saw it in the loss of speed during the five-mile runs. He took me aside and surprisingly sent me to get it checked. Quickly after, he shared with me that there was no shame in taking an honorable discharge for physical reasons. The army had instilled in me the discipline my godfather said I lacked, the notions on how life really worked, and taught me that if I wanted to thrive, I had to learn the rules to navigate and win.

Being in the armed forces changed me so much that after getting out, I went back to night school to get my high school diploma. I was fortunate enough to have great teachers who encouraged me to go to college, and the rest is history. I graduated in 1984 with a bachelor's degree in business from Bishop's University and in 1988 with a M.Sc. in computer science from Montreal University. To this day, I truly believe that my dad was there every step of the way and it was he who kept me motivated to push as far as I could.

My business career started somewhere between the BBA and the M.Sc. Just before I left Bishop's University, a student that I had never noticed before approached me and asked if I could help his uncle select a computer for his business. I was, after all, the student in charge of the computer center. I quickly responded that I would gladly help. The student's name was Steven and I told him that I would be in Montreal in approximately two weeks, would be staying at the Montreal University residence, and that he could reach me through the front desk as my phone would be activated within a few days after arrival.

An unbelievable sequence of events followed Steven's call. He came to pick me up because his uncle's business was so far away, I actually wondered on the way if it even figured on any map. St. Calixte, QC was where the business was located. When we first arrived, I looked skeptically at a house covered with painted particle boards—definitely not what I was expecting. Nonetheless, we went inside and there was a receptionist, a draftsman, and six shop workers. We looked around for almost forty-five minutes before Mr. Cousin (Phil) had time to sit down with us. Phil was a tall gentleman with piecing blue eyes, very handsome, and he had an impressive personality. He muttered out in a firm voice, "What kind of computer do we need?" I quickly replied that if he were to buy a computer right now, he would most likely be bankrupt within a few years. He was on his feet within a nanosecond, shouting and moving in our direction, frantically helping us out the door. I had not felt fear since I had gotten in the army, but on the way out, I dared shout back, "Look at the big plate with the two screws: Your cost is underestimated by thirty percent!" We quickly left and once we were back in the car, I commented to Stephen that I thought his uncle was a nut-case. It was a few years later when I learned the reason he reacted so strongly was that he had gone bankrupt many times before starting this last business.

Two months passed and I was well into my studies when all of a sudden, the phone rang. "Hello, it's Phil, do you remember me?"

"Yes, of course Mr. Cousin," I replied.

He asked me if I had time for breakfast, and being a student with very little means, I quickly accepted the offer, "Tomorrow? Alright."

Phil offered to pick me up where Steven had picked me up the last time.

The following day, we drove to a nearby restaurant and to my dismay, we ordered breakfast and not a word was spoken until breakfast was over. After what seemed like an eternity, he slowly pushed his plate away, looked at me and said, "How were you able to pick up that I was missing thirty percent on an outside division plate?"

Obviously, I said I knew nothing of that reference.

He added, "The big plate with the two screws, how did you know?"

I slowly and carefully replied, "Well I could charge you a fortune for this, but I will tell you no charge." I laughed a bit and continued, "Out of the three workers that seemed to be spending roughly the same amount of time, only two took the time to go to the time clock and enter the time they spent working on those parts. Two out of three—I just kept a safety margin."

He quickly jumped in, asking who was the culprit who'd skipped entering his time, which I obviously did not remember. Instead, I offered that the problem wasn't the workers, it was the system that did not allow a cross-check between time entered on jobs and time paid. After the explanation, he took me back to the residence and left without saying much more.

Another surprising call came in a month later. The phone rang and guess who was on the line? It was Mr. Cousin with another request to have breakfast together. "Call me Phil," he said in his big voice. We went to the same restaurant and followed the same routine as the previous time. After breakfast, he slowly pushed his plate away and looked at me, stating, "You are a smart guy, would you develop the system you think we need to improve our costing system?"

I said, "I would have to think about it, but if I could do it inside my curriculum, it could be done."

"What would you charge me?" he demanded.

"I would require a car and gas, and when I am working in St. Calixte, you need to pick up the food."

"Let me know," he replied. With his promise of a car, gas, and food, I called him back the next day to give him the good news that I would help him. "When do you start?" he asked.

I replied that I could start as soon as I got the car, to which he answered he had rented a brand new VW Jetta diesel. "I hope you like silver, it was the best deal they had."

Silver it was, and the following week I found myself back in St. Calixte, Quebec on my first day of a venture that lasted over twenty years.

I continued to work with Phil and together, we built a great business from almost nothing. When he turned sixty-five, a surprising coincidence changed both of our lives. Bartley Company announced that they were going to close their manufacturing division in Toronto, Ontario. Bartley was the largest concrete machinery manufacturer at the time. Based out of Alpena, Michigan, they were an impressive company. Phil felt that he had taken enough risks in his life and that it was time perhaps to sell the company and cash out. When I had joined him as a partner and bought fifty percent of the company for next to nothing, I had promised that when the time came for him to sell, I would not be an obstacle.

We did sell, and I became Bartley-Canada's president. Under Jerry, the president and owner of Bartley Company, we grew the business threefold and until Jerry retired, we had the happiest team you could ever find. When Jerry retired, I did not get along with the new management. Within a few short months the happiness that had taken so long to build was all but gone. It was with great emotion that I decided to leave and seek a place where I could again find what had just been taken away from me and all the workers at that plant.

Pursuing my career in the concrete industry, I bought twenty percent of the shares in Techniseal and became its president. It was my wish to replicate what I had developed at my previous company. Creating an environment where people can create happiness for themselves and their surroundings is the greatest feeling any leader can experience. It is a long process, but in the end, it is well worth the effort. Seeing people work hard because they love their jobs is the most rewarding feeling I have ever felt. Furthermore, rewarding someone for a job well done is also very rewarding.

History has repeated itself, however, and after more than fifteen years as an owner-operator, the company was sold to CRH, an Ireland-based company that made an offer we couldn't refuse. At the time of this writing, I had spent over seventeen years at the helm of Techniseal and I had been proud of every moment. My role expanded well into the CRH structure and my contribution spread across many divisions that CRH owns in the US and Europe before I decided to concentrate my time and effort in writing this book and building Fun2Work.

Exhibit A – The Lesson of the Concubines

The following story is considered to be of dubious authenticity and not part of the thirteen chapters of Sun Tzu's *The Art of War*. Some translators include it within their books; others ignore its existence. All the narratives are quite similar. You may find interesting lessons in the following version.

Sun Tzu's book, *The Art of War*, earned him an audience with the king of Wu, who said, "I have thoroughly read your thirteen chapters. May I submit your theory of managing soldiers to a small test?"

Sun Tzu replied, "Sir, you may."

The king of Wu asked, "Can the test be applied to women?"

Sun Tzu replied that it could, so arrangements were made to bring 180 beautiful women from the palace. Sun Tzu divided them into two companies with one of the king's favorite concubines at the head of each. He then made all of them take spears in their hands and spoke to them: "I presume you know the difference between the front and back, right hand, and left hand?"

The women replied, "Yes."

Sun Tzu continued, "When to the sound of drums I order 'eyes front,' look straight ahead. When I order 'left turn,' face toward your left hand. When I order 'right turn,' face toward your right hand. When I order 'about turn,' face around to the back."

After the words of command had been explained, the women agreed they understood. He gave them spears so he could begin the drill. To the sound of drums, Sun Tzu ordered, "Right turn."

In response, the women burst out in laughter.

With great patience, Sun Tzu said, "If the instructions and words of command are not clear and distinct, if orders are not thoroughly understood, then the general is to blame." He then repeated the explanations several times. This time he ordered the drums to signal "Left turn," and again the women burst into laughter.

Then Sun Tzu said, "If the instructions and words of command are not clear and distinct, if orders are not thoroughly understood, the general is to blame. But if commands are clear and the soldiers disobey, then it is the fault of the officers." He immediately ordered the women who were at the head of the two companies to be beheaded.

Of course, the king was watching from a raised pavilion, and when he saw that his two favorite concubines were about to be executed, he was alarmed and swiftly sent down a message: "We are now quite satisfied as to the general's ability to manage troops. Without these concubines, my food and drink will not taste good. It is the king's wish that they not be beheaded."

Sun Tzu replied, "Having received the sovereign's commission to take charge and direct these troops, there are certain orders I cannot accept." He immediately had the two concubines beheaded as an example and appointed the two next in line as the new leaders.

Now the drums were sounded again and the drill began. The women performed all the maneuvers exactly as commanded, turning to the right or left, marching ahead, turning around, kneeling, or rising. They drilled perfectly in precision and did not utter a single sound.

Sun Tzu sent a message to the king of Wu saying, "Your Majesty, the soldiers are now correctly drilled and perfectly disciplined. They are ready for your inspection. Put them to any use you desire.

As sovereign, you may choose to require them to go through fire and water and they will not disobey."

The king responded, "Our commander should cease the drill and return to his camp. We do not wish to come down and inspect the troops."

With great calm, Sun Tzu said, "This king is only fond of words and cannot carry them into deeds."

Commentary following the story indicates that the King relented, recognized Sun Tzu's ability, and appointed him a general; and Sun Tzu won many battles. In contrast, some historians believe Sun Tzu simply served as a civilian strategist, and others deny his existence, claiming he was actually someone else.

The moral of the story could be a lesson on training, discipline, command structure, role playing, or perhaps job interviews. The thoughtful reader may use his or her imagination to determine applicable lessons.

Exhibit B – The Seven Pots of Gold

Once there was a barber who was doing his duty for the king. The king was generously giving him one gold coin for every day of his work. The barber was definitely in a better financial position when compared to his clan. However, he felt that he should have more riches in life. One day, when he was journeying in the forest, he heard a voice of a Yaksha (a holy angel) telling him, "O barber, do not worry. Go back to your house, you will see seven pots of gold coins!"

The barber became very happy and quickly rushed to his house. There were seven pots. But gold only half-filled in the seventh pot. In other words, he had six and a half pots of gold.

He was a little disappointed. Anyhow, he decided to fill in the seventh pot with his royal income. He continued his work with the king, and placed in one coin every day, without eating, without proper clothes, and not caring for his wife and children. Still the seventh pot did not come to the brim. This continued for some more weeks. The barber became morose. While he was working for the king, the king noticed his melancholy. *In spite of good royal income, this fellow is not happy. Why?* wondered the king.

One day, the king asked the barber what was wrong. The barber said, "Nothing, sir!"

The king said, "I know. Have you also got seven pots of gold from the Yaksha?"

The barber was surprised.

The king continued, "Yes. I also got seven pots from Yaksha. But one pot was not full. I started saving and putting gold coins into that pot but that pot never got to the brim. The only result was that I became melancholic in life, asking for more and more gold coins from the citizens as tax. One day, I went to the Yaksha and returned the seven pots. From that day, I became quite happy. Go and throw back the seven pots to the Yaksha. You will become happy in life!"

Our search for the happiness in the world is also like this. We want a good job. Then we want a good wife. Then good children. Then their weddings. One day, we get struck with illnesses and senility. We want health. We definitely want long life without death. Our search and attainment gives only more discontent, and further search, which is futile after some time.

Do not depend on happiness from the world. Depend on Bhagavan Ramana or any Guru or God and you will attain happiness. You continue your search for the world's happiness to a minimum extent and be content with what you get!

(From Brahmasri Nochur's Satsangh)

Arunachala Siva.

Exhibit C – Speech by Michel Caron December 2010

Speech made by Michel Caron on December 1, 2010 at St-Jean Royal Military College

I would like welcome Jacques Tremblay, my previous business associate at Tremca Group, with whom I spent many wonderful years.
   Mr. Mayor and Prefect Gilles Dolbec
   Ladies and Gentlemen Councillors
   Ladies and Gentlemen, Presidents of Organizations
   Mr. President of the House,
   To you all, hello.
   It was my birthday Monday—already sixty-six years. Whether this conference is good or bad, you will not have wasted your time, as your presence here today gives me the energy to survive a long time. You are giving me a real gift, a real dose of adrenaline.
   Seated like this, we are less nervous, and even more, it is less apparent that I'm not tall. Even if my voice is less strong than it was before, it is with much enthusiasm that I address you here today. I am honored to have been invited as a speaker, and I thank the Chamber of Commerce and Vie Autonome Montérégie for this invitation. I am profoundly touched to see you here in such large numbers and I will do everything possible to make sure you don't leave here with the impression that you wasted your time.

I hesitated a lot before accepting the invitation because I'm not comfortable speaking in public, but even more so because it's a delicate topic with which I have barely a year of experience.

At my last lecture, I had lost thirty pounds. This time, I have probably shortened by an inch. So, what I hope to accomplish this afternoon, is simply to share with you my experience and especially my personal thoughts since the accident that changed my life.

I have three topics which I would like to speak of this afternoon.

The first is that it's not because we are handicapped that we have no more abilities, no more projects, no more ambitions and no more fun.

The second is the importance of integrating more handicapped people in our workplaces.

And the third topic is a bit more personal and it revolves more around what my accident made me realize about the priorities in my life.

So, my first topic: It's not because we are handicapped that we have no more abilities, no more projects, no more ambitions, and no more fun.

When we speak about seeing beyond disability, it's because there is something to see. To further explain my point, I will tell you about myself and people's perception of me. And if it's true for me, it's probably true for many others.

Mona, would you please stand up?

Do you think I am lucky to have such a beautiful and kind woman by my side? Do you know how many times I have been told that I'm lucky to have Mona by my side? A hundred times maybe. Plus all of you—another 700! Before my accident, I spent seventeen years with Mona and I was never told that I was lucky to have her by my side. It's like I have nothing more to offer her. That she is with me out of pity. Maybe I still have a little charm even if I'm in a wheelchair? Maybe I'm still interesting? This summer, I was at the Nautique and a beautiful girl leaned over me to say that she found me attractive. You may say she has no taste! That she was drunk! But maybe I'm still attractive. Between you and me, even if I am attractive, I am still so lucky to have Mona. You will understand why later.

Let's speak of my cars.

My cars are not for sale. Stop calling me to see if they are. The answer is no. It's not because I'm in a wheelchair that I have no more interest in cars. Believe me, I will find a way to use them soon. Since my accident, I have already visited two car shows. But I have also visited a showroom of wheelchairs. Anyway, I already have five. Maybe I will start to like that.

Also stop calling me to offer me work or projects. I am not looking for a job. I am not retired. Stop worrying that I'm bored. I still have my companies, exactly like before. I am involved with Tremca, which is now Armtec. I visit my company in Gatineau every month. I take advantage of greeting Denis Hébert and Alexis Loisel, our great partners in this wonderful venture. I also visit my company in New Jersey every month. And I have even gone back to visiting my companies in Florida. It's a bit complicated to take the plane, but we work it out.

Recently, I was visiting my father in a convalescent home and in the same room as me was a very old woman. I saw her use all her energy just to stand up, walk slowly toward me and with a trembling hand, she touched my hand and said in my ear: I will pray for you. And yes, I responded that it is probably preferable that I pray for her!

But even worse than that. A reflex that many people have around me, and that must be the case for other disabled people too, is to conclude that because I'm in a wheelchair, I'm disabled everywhere! You would be surprised at the number of times I ask someone a question and they respond directly to Mona without even looking at me. Hello! What's the deal! I'm here!

Do you see where I'm coming from? Because I'm in a wheelchair, people assume consciously or unconsciously that I no longer have interests, abilities, motivations, ambitions. Well, that's not the case for me or for other people with disabilities. You know, we the disabled, have the same abilities, means, ambitions, potential as everyone else. You will not make me say that we are not beautiful and not nice. We just need a suitable environment. We have as much to offer as anyone else.

Which brings me to my second topic: The importance of integrating handicapped people in our workplaces.

Before my accident, my attitude towards handicapped people was probably the same as many of us here. That is to say, a good attitude overall, but it was not something I had spent a lot of time thinking about. Of course, I never parked in the disabled areas. Besides, it made me angry when someone did. I always said it was the best way to become disabled. When an elevator arrived, I was polite and always let someone in a wheelchair or crutches get on first.

I offered a hand whenever I could help. I was also one of the best at selling tickets for a brunch for handicapped people. Thank you to all those who buy tickets year after year. If you allow me, I will sell them again next year. I also gave money occasionally. But I was also guilty of doing the same things that I blame many today for doing. I thought someone in a wheelchair meant that person was unhappy, helpless. When I met someone who was dynamic, I was surprised.

Believe me, I realized today that the majority are. I did so little in the background that in my own business in Iberville, I did not even have a ramp for the disabled, nor did I have reserved parking. And I did not have any disabled employees in my company. Not because I did not want to do it, but because it never crossed my mind.

It's hard enough to have a disability, and I'm in a good position to confirm that if you cannot find a job, it can become incredibly boring. Because for a person, whether disabled or not, a job is what's most important. It is with that, that we realize ourselves, that we value ourselves. Work is life.

When I ask you to make an effort and hire a disabled person, it is not charity that I am asking of you. It is not the handicapped people I am trying to help, it's you!

People with disabilities have a lot to offer an employer. I would say that often we have more to offer than a person without a disability. Because our disability forces us to see life differently, to organize differently, to become more creative, to think differently. All experts agree on the importance of diversity in a team. It's important for a company to have people with different backgrounds, and different experiences.

And that's not all. All we hear today is how difficult it is to find good people. All employers will agree with me that it is increasingly difficult to find competent, loyal, creative, reliable staff. Well, would not it be time to look at people with disabilities a bit more? What are we waiting for? In any case, I started: We are in the process of hiring one in my company in Florida. And I have a disabled ramp in Iberville as well as in Gatineau. The two most beautiful ramps in the world, and also nice reserved parking.

Having said that, there are always two sides to a coin.

The disabled also have their job to do. Now that there are companies ready to hire you. Go at least knock on doors. They will not go and find you at your place. Do not be surprised to see many wheelchairs wandering the streets of Saint-Jean next week.

Me, I'm lucky, I have a job. I found one right away. To tell you the truth, it's the same one I had before. But this is not the case for all people with disabilities. So, ladies and gentlemen in business: Why not hire a disabled person? I honestly think that more often than not, it's just because we did not think about it. Unfortunately, it is probably also because we have prejudices, consciously or unconsciously. It's hard to see beyond disability. So, I say to you: Let's think about it, let's look at how we can better integrate these individuals.

Sometimes, all it takes to change a life is to have a chance to show what you can do. The concept of giving someone a chance applies to a lot of situations, I'm not just talking about people with disabilities. I am the perfect example of a guy who had a chance. When I went into business in the late '70s, five guys trusted me by signing for a loan at the bank. By the way, I greeted a few earlier. Thanks guys. See what it has given! Of course, you have to know how to grab your chance, but to grab it, someone has to offer you the chance. It's a bit like that with people with disabilities. Many have so much to offer. They just need a chance to prove it.

Finally, my third topic, as I mentioned earlier, is a bit more personal and concerns what my accident made me realize about the priorities in my life.

Everything is a question of perspective. Is my situation easy? Of course not. In addition to losing the use of my legs and arms, I lost my father last month, one of my associates in New Jersey, and one of my dogs recently (Raoule was a girl). As they say, it will not be easy. But I have a choice to make. What do I want to leave as a legacy? It is well known in the family business that my sons take care of the income, and me the expenses. So, since I may be spending all my money, I thought of leaving something else for their inheritance: A happy old man in a wheelchair. That way, when they have a bad day, they will only have to think of me.

Despite the bad luck of my accident, I'm very lucky. I am still alive. It didn't affect my brain. I have the financial means to organize myself well. And I have a lot of people around me who love me and who are there to help me. This is unfortunately not always the case for people in my condition. And the lack of resources, financial or human, can often complicate situations that are already very difficult. At the Montreal Rehabilitation Institute (MRI), I saw patients delaying their release because they had no money, and no rent.

So I am lucky. And when something like that happens to us, we can only question ourselves and ask ourselves big questions. For me, my accident allowed me to better realize what a wonderful family I have. Five beautiful grandchildren, three of whom I now see often, who are here today. One thing is certain, I had not appreciated my family enough. I had other priorities. I was too busy to realize what I had, to see it. Sometimes you know, we create needs for ourselves—we imagine that it takes all kinds of things to be happy.

And one day, we realize that it's more simple than that, that we complicate it for nothing. That basic happiness comes from the little things. But also from nice cars! So, I intend to go and see the Rondeau brothers to buy myself a nice Fiat, Ferrari-red, with a red interior also.

You know, I spent sixty-five years dealing with a crazy man. Finally, I managed to catch him. He lost his legs and arms, but not his head. He's still crazy, but he's easier to control. And he has begun to realize things.

Conclusion: One thing I want to say before concluding is that today I told you about my experience, but there are many stories of courage, perseverance, determination that are plenty more impressive than mine. You only have to look around you. I want to emphasize this courage and determination that many people in similar situations, or even more difficult than mine, have demonstrated.

There are many examples, even at home. People like Jean-Paul Normandin, and many others. People who have done very well in business. People who have managed to keep their morale high. People who have accepted their situation and do their best every day. Often with much more modest means than mine. Those people are the real champions.

I will end with thanks.

I cannot possibly name all those who helped me and are still helping me with their love, their support, their presence. I would be too afraid to forget someone. But you know who you are, and I sincerely thank you. But I must still point out certain people:

Mona, my better half, thank you for everything. I am very happy to have you in my life. Without you, I wouldn't be here today. She's my angel. She does everything I can't do. She makes me eat and drink. She dresses me to go out. She speaks to me and listens to me. She undresses me and puts me to bed. She wakes up during the night to turn me over. She drives, sometimes for an entire day, to bring me to my shop in New Jersey. She even scratches my nose for me!

Claire, the mother of my two sons, who I know is very sad to not be here today, because she is on a trip that was organized a long time ago.

Eric and Hugues, my two sons. Less than thirty-six hours after my accident, my two sons and their wives, Sylvie and Caterina, were already by my side. I would not have survived without them, or without that gang of Italians and a neck brace. My first words were: Get me out of here before I die! And so, my two sons had already become lawyers. They negotiated with the doctor to get me released, and they negotiated with me to get me to wait. Ten days later, I was in a plane. I was lucky, I told you: I have two hard-working and intelligent sons. Genetics are pretty strong! They were already taking very good care of the companies before my accident, it is even more true today. And if I were to die, the companies wouldn't even feel it. As I said hundreds of times to my friends, it's the best gift I have ever received from God.

Sylvie, my daughter-in-law, thank you for everything, and especially for your involvement when I was most in trouble, that is to say the first months. I know from Eric that in Italy, you made the difference. Not to mention all the preparation work you did for my first outing at home, etc.

My grandchildren; Alexandre, Katherine, Gabrielle, Michael, and Sophia that I adore. Alex, Katherine, Gaby, stand up please. Thank you for your frequent visits. When you arrive, it turns me upside down. I see you becoming wonderful adults. There was me, then things improved with Eric and Hugues, and things will improve even more with your generation.

Billy and Myriam, who were with me when the accident happened – they surely saved my life.

June, who takes care of me every morning, my secretary. We are doing so much together. Thank you so much June.

Jean, my driver, my mechanic, my engineer, my innovator, thank you.

Claudette, my administrative assistant, thank you so much.

Francois Jovin and his team of physiotherapists, thank you.

Sonia, my esthetician, thank you.

My brothers and sisters, my sister-in-law, Nicole. Thank you Jacques, Francine, Nicole.

The team at Tremca. Thank you for your warm greetings. You are fantastic.

A special thank you to my friend and doctor, Luc Ouimet.

Thank you also and congratulations to the personnel from the CLSC—I hope there are some in the room.

Thank you all for being here today – you are more than 700, it touches me deeply. You will not have wasted your time this afternoon because you have given me a huge dose of encouragement for the future.

And I would be remiss not to mention also the work of all caregivers, all those who help a disabled person. It's not easy to be a disabled person. It's even less easy for those who help us. Talk to Mona!

Many wonder how I did not fall into a depression. Well, it's partly due to many of you. Among others: Baillargeon, Beaudin, Courville, Frégeau, Roy, Beaudry, Beauregard, Breton, Dorais, Doucet, Galipeau, Gaudette, Huet, Lange, Laguë, Paré, Petronius, Rajotte, Rathé, Paradis, Rioux ...And I could go on for a long time.

You never gave me two minutes of respite to allow me to be discouraged. Not two inches to become depressed. Not a day goes by where I am not visited by my family or friends. Continuous encouragement. Dinner at a restaurant. Christmas, New Year's Day, the holidays always with family. Hello Michel, don't give up Michel, you're getting better Michel, you're handsome Michel (I'll end up believing it's true!), you're making progress Michel, it's coming Michel, we're here for you Michel. How could I end up depressed? You don't give me the chance! So my success, it's you guys. And for that, I thank you.

I am smart enough to know that the battle has not been won. That the challenge is big. But it seems that our friend above sends us only what we are capable of handling. I think he has overestimated my abilities. He could have held back a little.

Thank you again.

Enjoy the rest of your meal and have a good afternoon.

Exhibit D – Who is Who

Dalai Lama — A title given by the Tibetan people for the foremost spiritual leader of the Gelug or "yellow hat" school of Tibetan Buddhism

Abraham Lincoln — American Statesman, lawyer who served as the 16th President of the United States

Buddha — A monk, sage, philosopher, teacher and religious leader on whose teaching Buddhism was founded

Florence Scovel Shinn — An American artist and book illustrator who became a new thought spiritual teacher and metaphysical writer

Elbert Hubbard — An American writer, publisher, artist and philosopher

Albert Einstein — A German-born theoretical physicist who developed the theory of relativity

Harry S. Truman — The 33rd President of the United States

Aristotle — A Greek philosopher during the classical period in ancient Greece

Confucius	A Chinese philosopher and politician of the Spring and Autumn period
Paul Greengard	An American neuroscientist best known for his work on molecular and cellular function of neurons
Glenn Wilson	Psychologist best known for his work on attitude and personality measurement
Pearl Strachan Hurd	1930s British Politician
Jack Canfield	American author, motivational speaker, corporate trainer and entrepreneur
Tony Robbins	An American author, philanthropist and life coach
Anatole France	A French poet, journalist and novelist with several best sellers
Marcus Aurelius	A Roman emperor and a stoic philosopher
George Sand	(Amantine Lucile Aurore Dupin) – Best known by her pen name George Sand, a French novelist, memorist and socialist
Martin Luther King	An American Baptist minister and activist who became the most visible spokesperson and leader in the civil rights movement

Jackson Brown Jr	An American author best know for his inspirational book Life's Little Instruction Book
Mahatma Gandhi	An Indian Lawyer, anti-colonial nationalist and political ethicist
Michael Jordan	An American former professional basketball player and principle owner of the Charlotte Hornets of the NBA
Lee Atwater	An American political consultant and strategist for the Republican Party
Steve Jobs	An American business magnet and inventor (Co-Founder of Apple)
Glenn Harold	British hypnotherapist and author of self-help books
Thich Nhat Hanh	A Vietnamese Buddhist Monk and peace activist
Eckhart Tolle	A spiritual teacher, a German born resident of Canada, best known as the author of *The Power of Now*
Pablo Picasso	A Spanish painter, sculptor, print maker, ceramicist stage designer and poet who spent most of his adult life in France
Jim Rohn	An American entrepreneur, author and motivational speaker

Albert Schweitzer	An Alsatian polymath. He was a theologian, organist, writer, humanitarian, philosopher and physician
The Beatles	English Rock band formed in Liverpool, England
Denis Waitley	An American motivational speaker, writer and consultant
Marcus Tullius Cicero	A Roman statement, orator, lawyer and philosopher
Lao Tzu	An ancient Chinese philosopher and writer
John Ortberg	An evangelical Christian author, speaker and senior pastor of Menlo Church
Wayne Dyer	An American self-help author and motivational speaker
Zig Ziglar	An American author, salesman and motivational speaker
Sun Tzu	A Chinese general, military strategist, writer and philosopher

CPSIA information can be obtained
at www.ICGtesting.com
Printed in the USA
LVHW092329160520
655731LV00001B/35